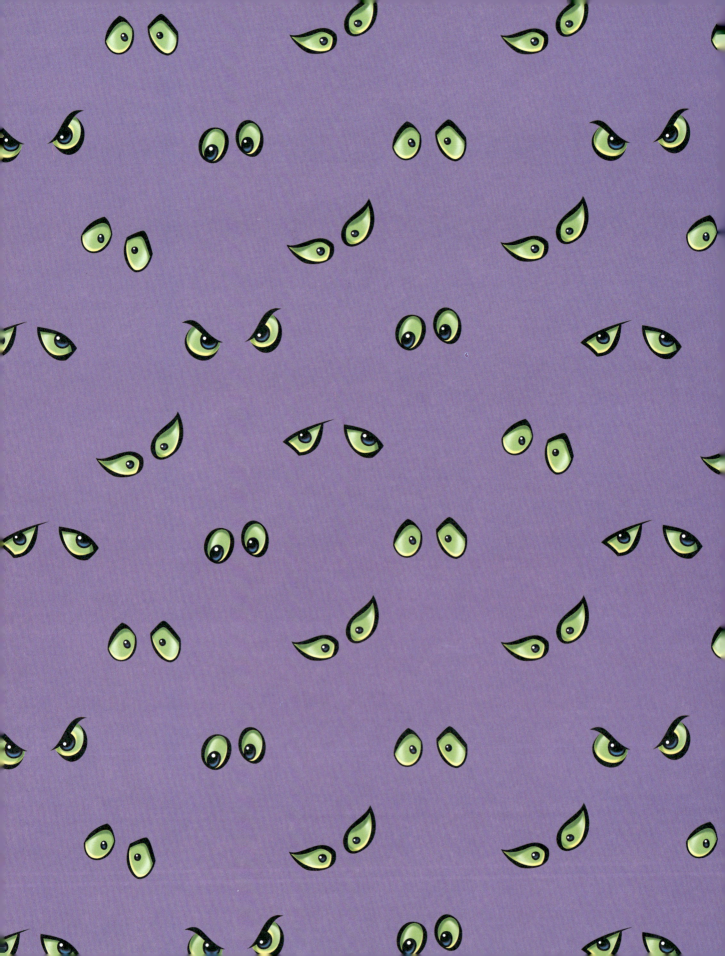

SCOOBY-DOO!
and the ATTACK of the SCOOBY SNACKS

RECIPES BY
ELENA P. CRAIG

WRITTEN BY
MARC SUMERAK

From Scooby Snacks and Pickled Vampire Wings
to Fried Moonbeams and More

INSIGHT EDITIONS

SAN RAFAEL · LOS ANGELES · LONDON

Contents

7 Introduction

Chapter 1: Snack Toppings

11 Double Dutch Chocolate Syrup
12 Sweet Cherry Relish
13 Bayou Pierre's Hot Sauce
15 Chocolate Covered Sardines
16 Toadstool Toppers
19 Mozzarella Skulls

Chapter 2: Snacks

22 Scooby Snacks
25 Scooby Snack Mix
26 Mellow Mutt Munchies
28 Secret Silo Popcorn
29 Chili Snacks
30 Pickled Vampire Wings
31 Werewolf Snacks, Chunky-Style
32 Fried Moonbeams
35 Spooky Layer Dip

Chapter 3: Side Snacks

38 Crawling Potato Beetles
40 Caprese Skull Salad
41 Super Garlic Food
42 Spicy Funky Fritters
43 Finger (and Toe) Fries
45 Eyeball Bites
46 Mummy Wrappings
49 Zucchini Zombies
50 Creepy Crab Brûlée

Chapter 4: Really BIG Snacks

54 C.R.U.S.T. Sticky Situation
56 Save Breakfast!
57 Ghost Pirate Stew
59 Sinister Spaghetti
60 Rizza Rie with Cherry Sauce
62 Stakeout? I'd Rather Have a Steak In!
63 Hex Fire Chili
65 Hot Dog Tacos with All the Trimmings
66 Jeepers! It's the Creeper Dog
69 Mini Burgers in a Pile

Chapter 5: Sandwich Snacks

- 72 Goth Bites
- 75 Super-Duper Hero Sandwich
- 79 Triple-Decker Veggie Club
- 81 Ham Sandwich (to Calm My Nerves)
- 82 Jaw-Stretcher Special
- 85 Hot Pepper Po' Boy

Chapter 6: Liquid Snacks

- 88 Scooby Shake (and Shiver)
- 91 Zoinks! It's a Shaggy Shake
- 92 Looks Like We Got Ourselves a Protein Shake
- 95 The Daphne
- 96 Jinkies! It's Thai Iced Tea
- 99 Like, It's Green, Like My Favorite Shirt
- 100 Countess Hagula's Youth Juice
- 101 Rock and Roll Ritual Tea
- 102 Cobweb Potion
- 103 Plain Iced Tea . . . If It Wasn't for You Muddling Kids!!
- 104 Bubbling Phantom

Chapter 7: Sweet Snacks

- 108 Fruitmeir's Ice Cream
- 111 Night Sky Tart with Bat Cookies
- 115 Spooky Haunted House Cake
- 120 A Trap Cake
- 125 Coffin Shaker Cookies
- 127 Jellied Eyeball Cobbler
- 128 Scooby-Doo Cookie Tags
- 130 Bat Macarons
- 132 Headless Horseman Pastries
- 135 It's a Clue! Panna Cotta

- 136 Suggested Menus
- 137 Measurement Conversions
- 138 Dietary Considerations
- 139 Fry Station Safety Tips
- 140 Index
- 143 About the Authors

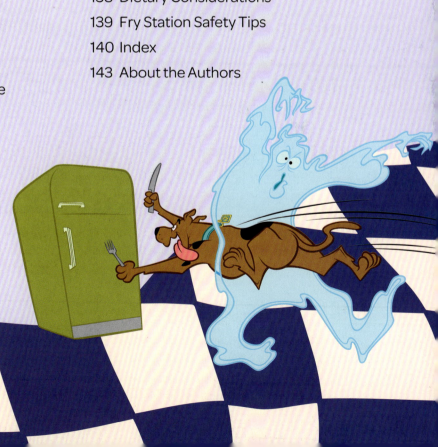

Introduction

Time to rev up the Mystery Machine!! Scooby and the gang are gearing up for one of their most exciting adventures yet, and you're invited to come along for the ride! It's the *Attack of the Scooby Snacks* and this case can only be solved by taking a culinary journey through some of the greatest recipes ever devoured by the members of Mystery Incorporated. Get ready for snacks of all sizes and flavors inspired by Fred, Daphne, Velma, Shaggy, and Scooby-Doo as well as a gallery of their greatest ghouls! Just follow the clues closely and you'll be led down a tantalizing trail toward a slew of sweet and savory solutions. Trust us, this is one caper you don't want to miss!

CHAPTER 1

Snack Toppings

When it comes to making the perfect snack, it's good to start at the top, or, in this case, the *toppings*! This selection of sauces and candies are used as components in countless recipes featured throughout these pages. So, the sooner you solve the mystery of how to make them, the better off you'll be!

Double Dutch Chocolate Syrup

Shaggy's never been shy about combining unexpected flavors when making a snack. He discovered long ago that a healthy squirt of chocolate sauce can take any dish to the next level. Add it to a super-sized sandwich or a big bowl of ice cream. Either way, these sweet and savory sauce variations make for groovy additions to your favorite treats!

Sweet

Yield: about 2 cups
V, V+, GF

½ cup unsweetened cocoa powder
½ cup unsweetened dark cocoa powder
1 cup dark brown sugar
½ cup granulated sugar
1 cup water

In a medium saucepan, over medium heat, combine the cocoa powders, brown sugar, granulated sugar, and water. Whisk thoroughly until completely smooth. Cook until the sauce comes to a gentle simmer. Cook for an additional 1 to 3 minutes or until it is thick enough to coat the back of a spoon. Remove from the heat and allow to cool for 15 minutes before transferring to a heat-proof container with an airtight lid. Store in the refrigerator for up to 2 weeks.

Enjoy with the Scooby Shake (and Shiver) (page 88), Cobweb Potion (page 102), or your favorite ice cream.

Savory

Yield: about 2 cups
V, V+, GF

¼ cup unsweetened cocoa powder
½ cup unsweetened dark cocoa powder
1 cup finely ground almond meal
½ cup molasses
2 chipotle peppers in adobo sauce, minced
1 teaspoon salt
½ teaspoon garlic powder
¼ teaspoon ground cumin
1 bay leaf
1 ½ cup water

SPECIAL TOOL
Immersion blender

In a medium saucepan, over medium heat, combine the regular and dark cocoa powders, almond meal, molasses, chipotle peppers, salt, garlic powder, cumin, bay leaf, and water. Cook until the mixture comes to a gentle simmer. Let the sauce continue to simmer, stirring constantly, until it is very thick, about 5 to 7 minutes.

Remove the pan from the heat and remove the bay leaf. Use an immersion blender to blend the sauce until it is silky and shiny, about 3 minutes. Return to the heat and simmer for 2 to 3 more minutes. Use immediately or allow to cool for 15 minutes before storing in a heat-proof container with an airtight lid. Store in the refrigerator for up to 2 weeks. Reheat in 30-second bursts in the microwave or in a saucepan over medium-low heat.

Enjoy with Hot Dog Tacos with All the Trimmings (page 65), Spooky Layer Dip (page 35), or any other place you might enjoy a spicy, smokey dip!

Sweet Cherry Relish

Yield: about 2 cups
V, V+, GF

When you travel around the world in a van with three other people and a giant dog, you learn quickly that storage space is extremely limited. That's why it's important to have multipurpose condiments on hand. This sweet and spicy cherry spread goes well with everything from pizza to cake. It does double duty for double the yum!

10 ounces pitted cherries, fresh or defrosted
1 teaspoon blood orange zest, see note
2 tablespoons blood orange juice, see note
⅔ cup granulated sugar
¼ teaspoon cayenne pepper
½ teaspoon five-spice powder

SPECIAL TOOL
Food processor

In the bowl of a food processor, pulse the cherries until they are roughly chopped.

In a medium saucepan, over medium-high heat, combine the chopped cherries and their juice, blood orange zest and juice, sugar, cayenne pepper, and five spice. Bring to a boil, then reduce to a simmer. Continue to cook, stirring frequently until reduced by ⅓ and the sauce is thick enough to hold a mound on the spoon, about 25 to 30 minutes.

> **TIP:** Turning on a hood exhaust fan while cooking can speed up this process.

Remove from the heat and allow to cool for 10 minutes before storing in an airtight container and refrigerate until needed. This can last in the refrigerator for up to 1 week.

Enjoy with Mummy Wrappings (page 46), Mini Burgers in a Pile (page 69), Hot Dog Tacos with All the Trimmings (page 65), Ham Sandwich (to Calm My Nerves) (page 81), Spooky Haunted House Cake (page 115), and Jellied Eyeball Cobbler (page 127).

NOTE: If blood oranges aren't available, then Cara Cara oranges make a great substitute.

Bayou Pierre's Hot Sauce

Yield: about 1 ½ cups
V, V+, GF

Down in New Orleans, Bayou Pierre used a blisteringly hot swamp pepper to make his line of hot sauces. Shaggy and Scooby put each other's taste buds to the test, sampling every heat level from "Flame 'N' Fortune" to "The Grim ReaPepper." This recipe's hotness lands right in the middle of Bayou Pierre's mouth-dynamite selections.

1 pound red chile peppers, such as fresh cayenne, red jalapeño, and/or red serrano

½ cup white wine vinegar

½ cup distilled white vinegar

1 to 3 tablespoons water

½ to 1 teaspoon salt

SPECIAL TOOLS
Food processor
Fine-mesh strainer

Seed and roughly chop peppers, discarding the stems. In a heavy-bottomed saucepan, over medium-high heat, combine the peppers and vinegars and bring to a quick boil. Reduce heat and simmer until peppers soften, about 10 minutes.

Cool pepper mixture slightly, about 10 minutes, and add to the bowl of a food processor. Process until smooth. If too thick, add water one tablespoon at a time and continue to process. Add in ½ teaspoon of the salt, stir well, taste, and adjust as needed.

Pour the mixture through a fine-mesh strainer to remove solids. Mix the hot sauce and store in an air-tight container or bottle. Refrigerate when not serving and it will keep for 1 to 2 months.

Enjoy with Spooky Layer Dip (page 35), Spicy Funky Fritters (page 42), and Hot Pepper Po' Boy (page 85).

NOTE: This hot sauce can be served right away but only gets better with time. Make this a few days or up to 1 week ahead.

SNACK TOPPINGS

Chocolate Covered Sardines

Yield: 24 fish
V, GF*

Sometimes you really want to order a pizza with extra sardines but Daphne doesn't want the meal to stink up the Mystery Machine while you're driving through a haunted forest. When that's the case, these sweet sardines are the next best thing! (Actually, they're probably the first best thing, but don't tell Shaggy!)

24 gummy fish
1 cup semi-sweet chocolate chips, divided
Sprinkles, optional
Silver or blue edible luster dust, optional

On a baking sheet covered in a silicone mat or parchment paper, lay out the fish and set aside.

In a microwave-safe bowl or measuring cup, heat ½ cup of the chocolate chips, in 30-second bursts, stirring in between. Once the chocolate chips are melted, add the additional ½ cup of chips. Using the residual heat, continue to stir until the mixture is smooth. If needed, microwave again for 10 seconds more.

Holding each fish by the tail, dip into the chocolate. Let the excess drip off and gently scrape on the edge of the bowl, to show some texture. Place back down on the baking sheet and dust with sprinkles, if using.

Once all the fish have been coated, place the baking sheet in the refrigerator until the chocolate is set, about 5 to 10 minutes. Brush each with luster dust, if using. (Note that the sardines shown at left are coated with luster dust.) Store in an airtight container for up to 2 weeks.

Enjoy with Like, It's Green, Like My Favorite Shirt (page 99), Scooby Snack Mix (page 25), or A Trap Cake (page 120).

NOTE: You can use milk chocolate or white chocolate to coat the fish or even drizzle a bit of contrasting chocolate across each one. *To make this recipe gluten free, use gluten-free gummy fish.

SNACK TOPPINGS 15

Toadstool Toppers

Yield: about 20 toadstools
V, GF

The best way to relax after being chased by monsters all day is with a light snack. And no snack is lighter than these crispy, airy toadstool meringues. Inspired by the unique recipes of Miss Grimwood, the headmistress of a finishing school for young ghouls, these mock mushrooms melt perfectly into a cup of spiced tea. You can also just munch on them by the handful!

3 egg whites

¾ cup sugar

⅛ teaspoon Kosher salt

¼ teaspoon orange or almond extract

⅛ teaspoon cream of tartar

About ½ teaspoon red powdered food coloring

About 1 tablespoon white nonpareils

½ cup white chocolate chips

Spiced black tea such as chai, for serving

SPECIAL TOOLS

Stand mixer fitted with a whisk attachment

Pastry bag fitted with a medium writing tip

Pastry bag fitted with a large writing tip

In a large pan (big enough to hold a mixing bowl) over medium heat, pour enough water to fill it up halfway.

In the bowl of a stand mixer, combine the egg whites, sugar, salt, and orange or almond extract. Place the bowl inside the pan of water and begin to whisk the mixture. Continue cooking and whisking until the mixture is shiny and thick, about 5 minutes. The mixture should be silky when rubbed between your fingers, without any sugar granules.

Preheat the oven to 200°F and line two baking sheets with parchment paper.

Transfer the bowl to the stand mixer. Add the cream of tartar and mix on medium high until stiff peaks form, up to 5 minutes. The bowl should begin to cool. Turn the speed to low and mix for another 2 to 3 minutes to finish cooling the mixture and remove any air bubbles.

Fit a pastry bag fitted with a medium-sized writing tip, about ¼ inch in diameter. Transfer ⅓ of the mixture to the bag. Secure the corners of the first parchment-lined baking sheet with a dot of meringue. Pipe the toadstool stems by holding the pastry bag vertical above the surface of the parchment. With strong pressure begin piping. Create a base about ½ inch in diameter. Ease up on the pressure as you lift up, making the ends tapered. Each stem should be about 1 inch tall. Pipe about 20 stems, spacing them about ½ inch apart.

Using the rest of the meringue, add the red food coloring and mix until the color is solid. Transfer the mixture into a second pastry bag fitted with a large writing tip, about ¾ inch in diameter. Secure corners on the second parchment-lined baking sheet and pipe about 20 mushroom-sized caps about 1 ½ inch in diameter. Sprinkle a few nonpareils onto each cap.

Bake for 45 minutes to an hour, or until the meringues feel very dry and light. Turn off the oven but keep the meringues inside, allowing them to cool completely.

Store in an airtight container until ready to assemble.

Melt the white chocolate chips in a microwave-safe bowl in 30-second bursts, stirring in between heat bursts until mixture is smooth. Use a small spatula to spread a thin layer of chocolate on the bottom of a mushroom cap. With a toothpick or small knife, score the spore lines into the chocolate. Dip the

thin end of a stem into the chocolate and stick it to the center of the cap. On a cutting board or baking sheet, place the mushrooms upside down, allowing the chocolate to set, between 5 and 7 minutes. Repeat with all the mushrooms.

TIP: You may find it helpful to cut a small piece of the narrow end of the stems off to create a flatter surface.

Once all the mushrooms have been assembled, store in an airtight container or package one or two in cellophane bags for gifting.

Enjoy these toadstools as the perfect sweetener for your favorite spiced tea! Use them as you would marshmallows for hot chocolate, to melt in your drink or pop right into your mouth!

Mozzarella Skulls

Yield: 20 skulls
V, GF

Want to make your salads look even more chilling or your pastas even more petrifying? These macabre Mozzarella Skulls can do the trick. This frightening fromage is easy to make and goes perfect in a Caprese Skull Salad (page 40) or on top of Sinister Spaghetti (page 59). They'll certainly be the talk of any ghoulish gathering, no bones about it!

20 fresh mozzarella balls, see tip
2 tablespoons balsamic glaze, optional
2 tablespoons balsamic vinegar, optional
1 tablespoon black or dark unsweetened cocoa, optional

SPECIAL TOOLS
Silicone skull mold
Paper towels or clean dish towels

Working in batches that match the number of cavities in your mold, place the mozzarella balls on a microwave-safe plate. Microwave for 20 seconds and dab dry. Press each mozzarella ball into each cavity of the mold. Using a clean paper towel or clean tea towel, press each mozzarella ball firmly into the mold, soaking up any excess liquid as you go.

TIP: The size that works best for this project is ⅓-ounce, cherry-sized balls, also called ciliegine.

Place the mold into the microwave and microwave for 10 seconds. Use the paper towel or tea towel again to remove any excess liquid and to continue to press the mozzarella balls against the surface of the mold.

Refrigerate the mold for 10 minutes.

Remove the mozzarella from the molds and place them into an airtight container. Refrigerate as you work the remaining batches.

To decorate and flavor the mozzarella skulls, plate them. Fill their eyes with balsamic glaze, toss the skulls in balsamic vinegar, or dust them with unsweetened cocoa powder for an all-over spooky look. Toss them in Dusk's Pesto (page 74) to create the Screaming Skulls of London monster!

Enjoy the skulls on a cheeseboard, a Caprese Skull Salad (page 40), or as a garnish for Sinister Spaghetti (page 59).

CHAPTER 2

Snacks

It's snack time!!! Of course, if you ask Shaggy and Scooby, snack time can be any time. Thankfully, with this selection of tasty treats, you'll be ready to chow down whenever the mood strikes! Whether you've got a craving for devilish dips, monstrous munchies, or just some old-fashioned Scooby Snacks, here are some perfect bites that won't bite back (we hope)!

Scooby Snacks

There aren't many things our pal Scooby-Doo wouldn't do for one of his signature Scooby-Snacks! These sweet, crunchy nuggets really keep him going when times get tough. Mystery Inc. probably blows most of their crime-solving budget on store-bought Scooby Snacks. You can use this top-secret recipe to bake up big batches, saving funds while saving the day!

Yield: about 120 snacks, with 40 of each flavor
V

¾ cup salted butter, softened
½ cup smooth peanut butter
¾ cup granulated sugar
1 egg
1 teaspoon vanilla extract
3 cups all-purpose flour
¼ cup mini chocolate chips
¾ teaspoon cinnamon
¼ cup marshmallow baking bits

SPECIAL TOOL
Stand mixer fitted with a paddle attachment or hand mixer

In the bowl of a stand mixer, or a large bowl if using a hand mixer, combine the butter, peanut butter, and sugar. Beat on high, until light and fluffy, about 2 to 3 minutes. Add in the egg and the vanilla, mixing again until incorporated.

Mixing on low, add the flour in three batches, until each addition is fully incorporated. If necessary, mix the last batch by hand.

Split the dough into three equal portions. Store each portion in separate medium bowls or airtight containers. To the first portion, mix in the chocolate chips. Add the cinnamon and marshmallow bits to the second portion. Leave the third portion as is. Cover each bowl or container with plastic wrap or lid and refrigerate for 20 minutes.

Working with one portion at a time, roll each flavor into a log, about 1 inch in diameter and about 6 inches long. Wrap each log in parchment and chill for another hour.

Preheat the oven to 350°F. Prepare two baking sheets with silicone baking mats or parchment paper.

Slice each log into ¼-inch slices and place close but not touching on the baking sheet. Use a finger to place a small indent in the center of each one. Bake for 7 to 9 minutes, or until just beginning to brown at the edges. Allow to cool completely on the baking sheet or a wire rack before storing in an airtight container for up to 1 week.

Enjoy as is, use as bribes, add to Like, It's Green, Like My Favorite Shirt (page 99), or use for Scooby Snack Mix (page 25).

Scooby Snack Mix

Yield: about 22 cups
V

One cannot live on Scooby Snacks alone. Okay, our pal Scoob definitely could. But adding a little variety to a diet never hurt anyone! This sweet-and-salty snack blend keeps that classic crunch while bringing some fun new flavors into the mix. It's made with popcorn, dried cherries, pretzels, nuts, and chocolate—and don't forget the Scooby Snacks! It's guaranteed to have you yelling "Scooby-Dooby-Doo!"

14 cups popped popcorn
2 cups salted mixed nuts or peanuts
2 cups mini pretzels
4 tablespoons ghee
1 tablespoon maple syrup
1 tablespoon soy sauce
¼ teaspoon five-spice powder
½ teaspoon vanilla paste
2 cups Scooby Snacks (page 22), broken into pieces
1 cup dried cherries
1 cup chocolate chunks or chocolate covered sardine pieces

Preheat the oven to 275°F.

In a large bowl combine the popcorn, nuts, and pretzels, and set aside.

In a microwave-safe bowl, combine the ghee, maple syrup, soy sauce, five spice, and vanilla paste. Heat for 30 to 45 seconds. Stir the ghee until melted and the ingredients are combined. Pour the ghee mixture over the popcorn mixture and stir until everything is completely coated.

Spread out onto the baking sheet, in a single layer, and bake for 15 minutes or until dry to the touch and fragrant.

In the same large bowl combine the Scooby Snacks and the cherries.

Remove the sheet from the oven and add the warm popcorn mixture to the bowl. Stir to combine. Allow the mixture to cool for about 5 minutes before stirring in the chocolate. Serve immediately or store in an airtight container for up to 1 week.

NOTE: If popping your own popcorn, start with about ½ cup kernels.

SNACKS   25

Mellow Mutt Munchies

Yield: 50 munchies
V*, GF*

When our favorite canine was just *A Pup Named Scooby-Doo*, he and Shaggy loved Commander Cool and Mellow Mutt! They may not have been real life superheroes, but that didn't make these comic-book characters any less, well, cool! Thanks to the marketing might of Colossal Toys, this crime-fighting duo became part of a branding bonanza, with their logos and likenesses on everything from action figures to these magnificent marshmallowy munchies!

3 cups puff rice cereal
½ teaspoon cinnamon
¼ cup confetti sprinkles
2 ¼ cups mini marshmallows
1 tablespoon heavy whipping cream
About 1 tablespoon unsalted butter for greasing, softened

In a large bowl, mix the rice cereal, cinnamon, and sprinkles. Stir to combine well and set aside.

In a microwave-safe bowl, combine the mini marshmallows and the heavy cream. Microwave for 1 minute and stir until completely melted. Add the cereal mixture all at once and stir until all the cereal is coated. Let stand for 2 to 3 minutes.

Prepare a large baking sheet with parchment paper or a silicone mat. Lightly grease your hands with a tiny amount of butter. Pinch off about 2 teaspoon–sized portions of cereal mixture and roll it into a tight ball and place on the sheet. Continue until all of the mixture has been formed. Let the balls set at room temperature for 15 minutes before serving. Store in an airtight container for 3 days.

NOTE: To make these munchies gluten free or vegetarian, choose gluten-free rice cereal and vegetarian marshmallows.

Secret Silo Popcorn

Yield: about 14 cups of popcorn
V, GF

Have you ever wanted the perfect popcorn recipe so badly that you were willing to dress up like a Demon Farmer, hop on a ghost tractor, and terrorize a litter of adorable puppies to get the code for a secret popcorn lab hidden in a farm silo? Well, fortunately, now you don't have to, thanks to this recipe inspired by one of the gang's most "Farmed & Dangerous" foes! Chew on that, Neville Poppenbacher!

4 ½ tablespoons ghee, divided
2 teaspoons salt, divided
2 teaspoons onion powder
½ teaspoon turmeric
½ cup popcorn kernels, popped, divided
1 tablespoon plus 1 teaspoon tomato powder
1 tablespoon chile-lime seasoning
1 teaspoon blue spirulina

In a large pot over medium-low heat, combine 1 ½ tablespoons of ghee, 1 teaspoon of salt, onion powder, and turmeric. When the ghee begins to melt, mix in ⅓ of the popcorn. Continue to cook for 1 to 2 minutes, stirring constantly until all the popcorn is well coated. Remove from the heat, transfer to a medium bowl, and wipe out the pot with a paper towel.

Return the pot to the heat, add another 1 ½ tablespoons of ghee, the remaining teaspoon of salt, and the tomato powder. When the ghee begins to melt, stir in another ⅓ of the popcorn and cook for 1 to 2 minutes, until well coated. Remove from the heat, transfer to another bowl, and wipe out the pot with a paper towel.

Return the pot to the heat and combine the remaining 1 ½ tablespoons of ghee, chile-lime seasoning, and the blue spirulina. When the ghee begins to melt, stir in the last ⅓ of the popcorn and cook for 1 to 2 minutes, until well coated. Remove from the heat and transfer to another bowl.

The popcorn can be served in separate bowls or mixed together for a fun presentation. Serve immediately or store in an airtight container for up to 3 days.

Chili Snacks

Yield: about 10 ounces
V, V+*, GF*

Mystery Inc.'s main mutt can't resist a scrumptious Scooby Snack, but another member of the Doo clan—Scooby's brother, Yabba-Doo—prefers a treat with a bit more heat. His best pal, Deputy Dusty, cooked up batches of these spicy snacks to give Yabba an extra boost as they protect the wild western town of Tumbleweed. You'll be hollerin' "Yippity-Yabbity-Doo!" after every blazing bite!

3 tablespoons avocado oil
1 teaspoon cayenne powder
¾ teaspoon chile powder
½ teaspoon onion powder
½ teaspoon garlic powder
¼ teaspoon cinnamon
12 fajita-sized corn tortillas, about 5 ½ inches
¾ teaspoon fine table salt, divided

Preheat the oven to 375°F.

In a small bowl, combine the oil, cayenne powder, chile powder, onion powder, garlic powder, and cinnamon.

Brush the oil mixture onto both sides of each tortilla. Make three cuts across each tortilla to create four strips and then cut the strips in half lengthwise.

On an ungreased rimmed baking sheet, place the strips in a single layer. Bake for 7 to 9 minutes until crispy and remove from the oven. Sprinkle with a ¼ teaspoon of the salt and toss the tortilla chips. Remove from the baking sheet and let the chips cool on a plate covered by a paper towel. Repeat until all strips are cooked. If you need to reuse a baking sheet, be sure to wipe it down before reusing.

Chips can be kept in an airtight container for up to a week.

Pickled Vampire Wings

Yield: about 6 cups
V, V+, GF

Shaggy and Scooby would've been batty if they'd eaten some of the things they found in the Franken Castle fridge while investigating "A Gaggle of Galloping Ghosts." But a look under Velma's magnifying glass reveals a shocking truth: These "vampire" wings are 100% bat-free! They're really just pickled kale with the right amount of bite to make them a perfect snack for vegetarian vamps everywhere!

2 bunches kale, Tuscan and/or red Russian

6 garlic cloves, divided

1 ½ teaspoons celery seed, divided

3 teaspoons coriander seeds, divided

6 teaspoons whole black peppercorn, divided

3 cinnamon sticks, divided

6 cups apple cider vinegar

4 cups water

2 tablespoons molasses

½ cup pickling salt or sea salt

SPECIAL TOOL

3 wide-mouth 24-ounce canning jars, sterilized, see note

Preheat the oven to 250°F.

Wash and dry the kale. Starting from the bottom, remove the toughest part of the stem. Move about halfway up each stalk, keeping the leaves at the top attached. Set the stemmed leaves aside and discard the removed stems.

Smash and peel the garlic cloves, placing two in each jar. Add ½ teaspoon of celery seed, 1 teaspoon coriander seeds, 2 teaspoons peppercorn, and 1 cinnamon stick to each jar. Place the jars on a baking sheet and put them in the oven for 10 minutes.

In a nonreactive pot, over medium-high heat, combine the apple cider vinegar, water, molasses, and salt. Bring to a boil, stirring to dissolve the salt. Boil for 1 minute and then remove from the heat.

Remove the jars from the oven. Using tongs, place the kale leaves into each jar until they are tightly packed. Fill each jar with pickling liquid until the leaves are submerged, leaving ¼-inch headspace at the top of each jar. You may have some extra liquid; discard or save for an alternate use.

Seal the jars with a tight-fitting lid and allow to cool to room temperature before refrigerating. The leaves can be enjoyed as soon as they cool but are best after 2 or 4 days. This can be stored in the refrigerator for up to 3 weeks.

Enjoy with a salad, on the Triple-Decker Veggie Club (page 79), or chopped up as garnish for Hot Dog Tacos with All the Trimmings (page 65), or Mini Burgers in a Pile (page 69).

NOTE: To sterilize jars, wash with hot soapy water or in the dishwasher. Place them on a baking sheet, mouth-side up, and bake them at 350°F for 10 minutes. They can cool down while you prepare the rest of the ingredients as long as they remain in the oven.

Werewolf Snacks, Chunky-Style

Yield: about 4 cups
GF

Another devilish delicacy found inside the frightening fridge of Franken Castle; these Werewolf Snacks certainly sound more terrifying than tasty. But this chunky chow is secretly a curried chicken salad that leaves all who eat it howling for more! Thankfully, you don't have to wait for a full moon to sink your teeth into this savory snack!

½ cup sour cream
2 tablespoons mayonnaise
1 ½ teaspoons curry powder
¼ teaspoon cayenne powder
¼ teaspoon garlic powder
12 ounces shredded chicken, see note
½ medium red onion, diced
½ cup diced dried apricot
½ cup lightly salted peanuts, roughly chopped
Freshly ground black pepper, to taste

In a small bowl, combine the sour cream, mayonnaise, curry powder, cayenne powder, and garlic powder.

Roughly chop the shredded chicken and add to a medium-sized bowl. Add the red onion, apricot, and peanuts. Add the sour cream mixture and stir until completely incorporated. Add the ground pepper to taste. Refrigerate in an airtight container until serving. This can be stored for 3 days.

Serve with crackers or a sliced baguette.

NOTE: Shredded chicken can be found in most grocery-store deli sections. You can also roast a chicken beforehand or buy a rotisserie chicken to shred later.

SNACKS   31

Fried Moonbeams

Yield: 8 sticks
V, GF

Franken Castle was a genuine Transylvanian fortress before it was taken apart brick-by-brick and rebuilt in America. While some may visit the castle in search of the legendary Franken Jewels, Shaggy and Scooby found a different kind of treasure inside: A fridge full of Transylvanian treats, including these stringy, crunchy, cheesy delights!

8 mozzarella cheese sticks, unwrapped

2 quarts frying oil, such as vegetable, peanut, canola, or safflower

¾ cup rice flour

¾ teaspoon salt

½ teaspoon oregano

1 teaspoon garlic powder

¾ cup sparkling water, very cold

Sinister Spaghetti sauce (page 59) or marinara, for dipping

Place unwrapped cheese sticks on a medium-sized baking sheet and freeze for 30 minutes.

In a large Dutch oven over high heat, or a deep fryer, bring the frying oil to 300°F. Once the oil has reached 300°F, begin to make the batter. See Fry Station Safety Tips, page 139.

In a large bowl, combine the rice flour, salt, oregano, and garlic powder. Add the cold sparkling water and stir until thoroughly mixed.

Working with one or two at a time, coat the frozen cheese sticks in the batter. When the oil is between 360°F and 365°F, lower the cheese into the hot oil. Fry until golden, turning gently with a spider skimmer for 2 to 3 minutes. Serve hot and immediately.

Spooky Layer Dip

Yield: 8 to 10 servings
V, GF

Ever feel like someone's watching you? Spend enough time with Scooby and the gang, and you're bound to see spooky eyes lurking in every shadow—and on every plate! This multi-layered dip may look like its olive eyes are glaring at you, but really, you should be the one watching it! Something this tasty is bound to disappear.

3 red bell peppers, stemmed, seeded, and quartered

2 tablespoons vegetable oil

1 teaspoon salt, divided

½ teaspoon freshly ground black pepper

One 14-ounce can whole black beans

½ teaspoon garlic powder

½ teaspoon onion powder

One 15-ounce jar Mexican crema

12 ounces pepper jack shredded, about 5 cups

1 to 2 tablespoons Bayou Pierre's Hot Sauce (page 13), optional

1 bunch green onions, thinly sliced

One 2.25-ounce can sliced black olives

30 ounces store-bought guacamole

½ lime, juiced

5 ounces blue-corn tortilla chips or Chili Snacks (page 29)

SPECIAL TOOLS

9-by-13-inch casserole dish

Food processor

Preheat the oven to 400°F.

In a roasting pan, toss the bell pepper with oil, ½ teaspoon of the salt, and pepper. Roast until the pepper skin starts to blister in places and they are tender, 15 to 20 minutes. Remove from the oven and allow to cool. After the peppers have cooled, cut them into ¼-inch pieces and set aside.

Drain both cans of beans.

In a large sauté pan, over medium heat, combine the beans, garlic powder, onion powder, and the remaining salt. Cook until the beans are warmed through, about 5 to 7 minutes. Remove the beans from the heat and lightly mash with a fork. Spread the beans into a 9-by-13-inch casserole dish, using a spatula to smooth the surface.

Pour the entire jar of crema across the surface of the beans and smooth with a spatula. Sprinkle the shredded cheese across the crema in an even layer. If using, shake hot sauce and drizzle across the layer of cheese. Sprinkle the green onions across the surface in an even layer. Place the cooled pepper pieces across in an even layer.

Drain the can of olives. Remove 10 to 12 olive ends and set aside. Sprinkle the remaining olives on top of the peppers. Gently press the cheese, onions, peppers, and olives down into the crema layer.

Mix the lime juice into the guacamole. Spread the dip in an even layer over the mixture. Smooth out the top with a spatula.

In the food processor, pulse the corn chips until finely ground. Top the guacamole with the chips, covering it completely.

Using a paring knife, carve two semicircles into the ground chips. Make sure the semicircles touch to make a set of eyes and keep the circle shallow to only reveal the green guacamole. Place the round ends of olives you set aside toward the top-inside corners of the guacamole semicircles.

The dip can be served immediately but is best when made a day ahead so the layers have a chance to set. Serve with your favorite corn chips, such as Chili Snacks (page 29), and extra hot sauce if desired.

SNACKS 35

CHAPTER 3
Side Snacks

Need another snack to go with your snack? Who doesn't?! No need to worry. Mystery Inc. has got your cravings covered! These sensational starters and sinister sides pair perfectly with any meal. From freaky fritters and fries to munchable monsters and mummies, this eerie assortment of apps and add-ons will help to flesh out any feast!

Crawling Potato Beetles

Yield: 16 beetles
V, GF

Mystery Inc. specializes in hunting ghosts and things that go bump in the night. They've also come into contact with their fair share of creepy crawlies along the way, from Giant Bees to a Cockroach Monster. Thankfully, these bite-sized bugs won't start skittering around and causing chaos. But a heaping bowlful might make your stomach squirm with delight!

1 medium carrot

16 mini gold potatoes, about 12 ounces, see note

4 tablespoons salted butter

1 garlic clove, minced

½ teaspoon finely ground black pepper

¾ teaspoon salt, divided

NOTE: Oval potatoes with a flattened side work best.

Preheat the oven to 400°F and line a baking sheet with parchment or a silicone mat.

Trim and peel the carrot, then julienne into strips approximately 2 ½ by ⅛ inches for the legs and antennae. You will need four pieces of carrot for each potato.

Working with one potato at a time, place it on a cutting board and in between two chopsticks. Using a paring knife, cut approximately ⅛-inch-wide cross-section slices, down the length of the potato. The chopsticks will prevent you from cutting through the potatoes, leaving the bottom intact. Place the sliced potatoes on the prepared baking sheet.

Melt the butter in a microwave-safe container and stir in garlic and pepper. Carefully open the potatoes slices and lightly baste with butter.

Place three carrot sticks in the bottom, middle, and top cuts of each potato to resemble legs. Poke two holes on the top of the potato. Slice a fourth carrot piece in half, shape the ends of each piece to a point, and place in the holes. This should resemble antennae. Repeat to assemble all the beetles.

Bake for 10 minutes, baste with more melted butter mixture, then bake for an additional 5 minutes.

Sprinkle with ½ of the salt and bake for another 5 to 10 minutes or until fork-tender.

Remove from the oven, baste a final time with the melted butter and broil on high for 5 minutes or until edges are crispy golden-brown. Remove from the oven, garnish with the remaining salt, and serve immediately.

Caprese Skull Salad

Yield: 4 servings
V, GF

Like any hungry hound, Scooby-Doo loves to sink his teeth into a big bone after a hard mission. Now, the rest of us can share in that joy, thanks to this classic caprese salad made with miniature Mozzarella Skulls (page 19)! It'll go perfectly a-*head* of any meal!

4 large, or 6 small, heirloom tomatoes, sliced

2 tablespoons olive oil

½ teaspoon sea salt or flake salt

Freshly ground black pepper, to taste

½ cup basil leaves, torn

1 tablespoon balsamic glaze, optional

20 Mozzarella Skulls (page 19), decorated as desired

Arrange the sliced tomatoes on a serving platter and drizzle with the olive oil. Sprinkle the salt and black pepper to taste. Scatter the torn basil over the platter and tuck the skulls into the spaces between the tomato slices. Serve immediately.

Super Garlic Food

Yield: about 12 skewers
GF

When vampires lurk in the night, it's good to have extra garlic on hand. Shaggy and Scooby once whipped up a garlic banana-berry shake and peanut butter and garlic cookies to help the Hex Girls fight against a menacing monster. This chile and sesame–marinated eggplant, served with a potent peanut sauce, is just as garlicky—and a lot more appetizing!

EGGPLANT SKEWERS
2 eggplants
1 tablespoon kosher salt
2 to 3 cups cold water or enough to cover the eggplant
¼ cup soy sauce
1 teaspoon fish sauce
1 teaspoon chile crisp
½ teaspoon sesame oil
½ teaspoon vegetable oil

PEANUT SAUCE
5 cloves garlic, diced
½ teaspoon sesame oil
¼ teaspoon vegetable oil
1 ½ teaspoons chile crisp
6 tablespoons coconut milk
½ lime, juiced
1 tablespoon soy sauce
3 tablespoons crunchy peanut butter
¼ cup warm water

SPECIAL TOOL
About 12 wooden skewers, soaked in water

To make the eggplant skewers: Trim the ends off each eggplant and slice them lengthwise, into ¼-inch slices. Cut each slice in half, again lengthwise. Place the slices into a large bowl or shallow casserole dish, cover them with water and stir in the salt. Soak the eggplant for 15 minutes and then transfer to a paper towel–lined surface to drain until dry.

While the eggplant is drying, preheat the oven, with two rimmed baking sheets inside, to 400°F.

In a large bowl, combine the soy sauce, fish sauce, chile crisp, sesame oil, and vegetable oil. Toss the dried eggplant in the marinade until it is well coated. Thread two to three slices onto each skewer, catching the slices in a few places to create a ribbon effect. Continue until all the eggplant is skewered. On the hot baking sheets, place the eggplant skewers and roast for 15 to 20 minutes or until tender and browning.

To make the peanut sauce: While the eggplant is roasting, mix together the garlic, sesame oil, and vegetable oil in a small saucepan, over medium heat. Cook until fragrant, about 3 minutes. Stir in the chile crisp, coconut milk, lime juice, and soy sauce and cook for another minute. Add the peanut butter and stir vigorously until incorporated. The mixture may look thick and curdled at this point. Remove the pan from the heat and slowly drizzle in the warm water, whisking as you go, until the mixture is smooth and the desired consistency.

Serve the skewers hot from the oven with small bowls of sauce or drizzle the sauce over the skewers.

Spicy Funky Fritters

Yield: about 20 fritters
V, GF

Want some of the fieriest fritters you can find? Head on down to Georgia's Hokeyfenokee Swamp and climb aboard the Skillett Showboat restaurant. Ma and Pa Skillett fry up these scorching hot dough balls for brave diners from far and wide. Pop a few in your mouth, and you'll see why Scooby's cousin, Scooby-Dum, thinks they're fab-u-lous! (As a bonus, the sticky batter is great for catching grimacing ghouls!)

JALAPEÑOS
- 3 tablespoons unsalted butter
- 1 tablespoon olive oil
- 5 jalapeños, seeded and diced
- 3 cloves garlic, minced
- ½ teaspoon salt
- Freshly ground black pepper, to taste

SPICY MUSTARD
- ¼ cup yellow mustard
- 1 tablespoon Bayou Pierre's Hot Sauce (page 13), plus more for serving, optional
- ½ teaspoon smoked paprika
- 1 teaspoon honey

BATTER
- 1 cup cornmeal
- ½ cup corn flour
- ½ cup rice flour
- ½ teaspoon baking soda
- 2 teaspoons baking powder
- ½ teaspoon kosher salt, plus more for finishing
- 1 cup milk of choice
- ¼ cup apple cider vinegar
- 2 eggs
- 2 quarts frying oil, such as vegetable, peanut, canola, or safflower

To make the jalapeños: In a small sauté pan, over medium heat, add the butter. When the butter begins to foam, add the olive oil and stir to combine. Add the jalapeño, garlic, salt, and pepper. Sauté until the peppers begin to soften and the garlic begins to brown, 2 to 3 minutes. Turn the heat down to low and continue to cook for another 2 to 3 minutes until the peppers color has darkened. Remove from the heat and set aside.

To make the spicy mustard: In a small bowl, mix together the mustard, hot sauce, paprika, and honey. Stir until smooth and set aside until serving.

To make the batter: In a medium bowl, mix the cornmeal, corn flour, rice flour, baking soda, baking powder, and salt together.

In a small bowl, combine the milk, vinegar, and eggs, whisking until well incorporated. Make a well in the dry ingredients, add the wet ingredients, and mix briefly, until just combined. Fold in the jalapeño-and-garlic mixture. Let sit for 15 to 20 minutes while bringing the oil up to temperature.

In a large Dutch oven, over medium-high heat, or deep fryer, bring the frying oil up to 365°F. Have a baking sheet fitted with a wire rack or lined with paper towels standing by. See Fry Station Safety Tips, page 139.

Using a 2-tablespoon scoop, add two or three fritters at a time to the oil. Fry for 30 to 45 seconds. Use a spider skimmer or metal tongs to turn over the fritters and fry for another 15 to 20 seconds. Remove to the baking sheet and sprinkle with salt. Continue with the remaining batter. Serve immediately with spicy mustard for dipping.

Finger (and Toe) Fries

Yield: 4 servings
V, V+, GF

For a truly gripping appetizer or side dish try these foreboding finger fries. Patrons of the vampire-themed restaurant called The Bloody Stake can't get enough of this creepy and crispy mix of fingerling potatoes. Be sure to make a few hands' worth, because one definitely won't be enough!

2 tablespoons olive oil
1 tablespoon balsamic vinegar
1 teaspoon kosher salt
1 teaspoon dried rosemary
1 ½ pounds fingerling potatoes

Place a rimmed baking sheet in the oven and preheat to 400°F.

In a large bowl, combine the olive oil, balsamic vinegar, salt, and rosemary.

Cut each potato in half lengthwise (or into quarters for very large potatoes) and use a paring knife to score a few "knuckles" into the length of the potato.

To create a nail bed, use the paring knife to remove a small portion of each potato from the narrowest end, just behind the tip. The nail bed should be about half of the thickness of the potato. After you finish each potato, toss them into the bowl and stir to coat.

Once the fingers are well coated, pour the potatoes and remaining dressing on the preheated baking sheet. You may need to shake or move the pan so the potatoes are in a single layer. Bake for 15 to 20 minutes or until the potatoes are fork-tender and well-browned.

Remove the pan from the oven. Shake to release the potatoes from the pan and remove with a spatula to a serving plate and serve immediately. Leftovers can be stored in an airtight container in the refrigerator for up to 3 days.

SIDE SNACKS 43

Eyeball Bites

Yield: 12 eye sockets or 6 servings
V

Jeepers creepers! Get a load of these peepers! The Spooky Layer Dip (page 35) isn't the only recipe with its eyes on you. These eerie eyeballs may look like they just popped out of their sockets, but with the time-tested combo of bananas and PB&J, you're not going to be able to resist popping them straight into your mouth!

4 slices buttermilk bread
2 tablespoons salted butter, divided
4 tablespoons strawberry jam, divided
½ teaspoon cinnamon, divided
About 4 tablespoons peanut butter or other nut butter
1 to 1 ½ large bananas
12 currants

SPECIAL TOOL
6 to 12 wooden skewers

Use a rolling pin to roll out each piece of bread to about ⅛-inch thickness. Trim off the top and bottom crust of each piece of bread. Cut each piece into three equal strips, lengthwise. You should have twelve strips.

In a large skillet over medium heat, combine half the butter, 2 teaspoons of jam, and ¼ teaspoon cinnamon. Stir continuously until the butter is melted. Add six strips to the pan and cook until most of the butter and jam has been absorbed and the bread is well-browned, about 3 to 4 minutes. Flip the bread over and brown on the other side for another 3 to 4 minutes. Remove to a cutting board.

Repeat step 2 with the second batch of bread strips.

Once all the bread strips have been browned, place them all on a cutting board, caramelized-side down. In a thin layer, spread the nut butter and remaining jam on each strip.

Slice the bananas to approximately the same width as each bread strip. Place a piece at one end of the bread, roll it up to the other end, and secure on a skewer. Press a currant in the center of each banana to create eyes. Repeat until all of the bread strips have been used. Serve immediately.

SIDE SNACKS

Mummy Wrappings

Yield: 4 to 6 servings
V*

First rule of monster hunting: If you open a sarcophagus, there's bound to be something scary inside. Of course there's an exception to every rule. This one happens to hide an entire cheeseboard within. You won't be able to resist raiding this tantalizing tomb. Don't forget to save some for your mummy!

MUMMY

13 to 15 sheets heavy-duty aluminum foil (if using aluminum foil from a roll, note that sheets are about 11-by-12-inches)

About 3 tablespoons coconut oil or cooking spray

1 egg plus 1 tablespoon water, for egg wash

One 17-ounce package puff pastry, thawed

About 2 tablespoons grated Parmesan cheese, optional

HIDDEN CHEESEBOARD

6 ounces Brie log, sliced

8 ounces mozzarella and prosciutto roll, sliced

4 ounces soft cheese bites

2 small bunches red grapes

Crackers for serving

½ recipe Sweet Cherry Relish (page 12), optional

NOTE: The cheeses suggested here are fun choices for their spooky look and ease of serving, but feel free to use the sarcophagus to hide anything you want, including vegetarian options. It's your tomb! The pastry can be made a day ahead and wrapped in plastic wrap or stored in an airtight container.

To make the mummy: Create the shape of the mummy's sarcophagus by balling up a sheet of foil to create the head. You can build this up by layering additional foil over the original ball. Roll four smaller balls to create the chest cavity. On a baking sheet covered with a silicone mat or parchment paper, place the head at the top of the pan, lengthwise. Place the four smaller balls, or the chest cavity, underneath.

Using the foil, create three oval shapes, with each one slightly larger. Using the smallest oval, lay the foil horizontally, underneath the chest area.

Using more foil, create two tube shapes to represent the arms, molding the foil to hold the shape. Place the arms under the head so they surround the chest area on either side.

Next create a long tube with the foil. Place the middle part of the tube at the bottom of the oval and wrap the foil up on either side. The foil does not need to meet with the arms. Now cover the entire structure with one large piece of foil, making the surface a smooth as possible and pressing it against the sides.

Brush or spray the entire shape with melted coconut oil or cooking spray, coating it generously. Remember to get all the nooks and crannies.

Preheat the oven to 400°F.

Whisk the egg and water together in a small bowl and have a pastry brush ready.

Unfold the pastry dough. Using a knife or a pastry wheel, begin to cut strips of puff pastry. They can be anywhere from ¼ inch to ¾ inch thick. The strips don't need to be even in shape.

Starting at the head, layer the strips across the foil structure. As you build the mummy wrap, egg wash each strip to help the pieces adhere. Continue until you have covered the form from top to bottom. Once the body is fully covered, trim off the excess around the entire structure. Use the excess pieces to fill where foil remains uncovered and to create the eyes. Brush the entire pastry with the remaining egg wash.

Chill for 10 minutes in the refrigerator before baking for 20 to 25 minutes or until golden-brown, crisp, and hollow-sounding when tapped.

Tip: Cover loosely with a sheet of foil halfway through cooking to keep from getting too dark.

Remove from the oven and immediately sprinkle with the Parmesan cheese, if using. Allow to cool completely on the baking sheet.

Once the pastry is cool, gently lift the structure and carefully pull the foil structure out of and away from the pastry shell. Once all the foil has been removed, gently lay the pastry back on the baking sheet.

To build the cheeseboard: Arrange the cheeses, grapes, and crackers in a narrow rectangular shape, about 6 by 18 inches. If using, place a small dish of Sweet Cherry Relish next to the board. Cover the cheese arrangement with the sarcophagus and serve. The strips of the mummy break away nicely and pair well with the relish and cheese.

SIDE SNACKS 47

Zucchini Zombies

Yield: about 20 zombies
V

Mystery Inc. has found itself face-to-face with countless frightening foes over the years. Even though each and every encounter has its mortifying moments, some menacing monsters are more memorable than others. These ghoulishly green pesto puff pastries pay homage to one of the classics, the Zombie. Just like this creature, they're sure to leave a lasting impression.

2 zucchini, halved lengthwise and seeded
½ teaspoon salt
½ cup basil leaves, minced
1 teaspoon lemon zest
2 tablespoons lemon juice
⅓ cup grated Parmesan cheese
One 17-ounce package puff pastry, thawed
1 egg plus 1 tablespoon water for egg wash
1 to 2 drops blue food coloring, optional
2 or 3 kalamata olives, pitted, optional

SPECIAL TOOLS
Cheese grater
Zombie cookie cutters

Using the large holes on a cheese grater, grate the zucchini into a large bowl. Add the salt and stir to combine. Let stand for 10 minutes. Using a fine-mesh strainer, drain the zucchini, pressing it into the mesh to release as much liquid as possible.

Discard the liquid and return the zucchini to the bowl. Add the basil, lemon zest, lemon juice, and Parmesan cheese. Stir to combine and set aside.

Preheat the oven to 400°F. Prepare two baking sheets with a silicone mat or parchment paper.

Working with one puff pastry sheet at a time, on a lightly floured surface, roll out the puff pastry to about 11 by 16 inches. Use the zombie cookie cutter to cut out as many zombies as possible.

Using the prepared baking sheets, spoon about 1 tablespoon of filling on the pan, creating rows of 3 by 4. Place a zombie pastry cutout on top of each filling pile, pressing gently to distribute the filling along the pastry. Using a fork, crimp the pastry all around the edges to the baking sheet. Repeat with the remaining zombies. Place the filled baking sheet in the refrigerator while you work with the second sheet.

Repeat the steps with the second sheet of puff pastry and chill the completed pastry for 10 minutes. Mix the egg and water together with the food coloring, if using. Brush each zombie with the egg wash and bake for 12 to 15 minutes, or until golden-brown and puffed.

While the pastries are baking, slice the olives to use as eyes.

Remove the pastries from the oven and allow to cool for a few minutes before flipping over with a thin spatula. Replace any dislodged filling, decorate with the olive strips, and serve warm or at room temperature.

Leftovers can be stored in an airtight container for up to 3 days.

SIDE SNACKS   49

Creepy Crab Brûlée

Yield: 6 servings

Being a member of Mystery Inc. is no day at the beach—unless you're on the beach to stop a mysterious Man-Crab from terrorizing tourists! A case like that works up an appetite, so unless you have a severe seafood allergy like Daphne, enjoy this delightful, deconstructed take on a crab cake in honor of Crystal Cove's criminal crustacean!

1 tablespoon olive oil
1 tablespoon salted butter
½ cup finely diced shallot
¼ cup finely diced bell pepper
¼ cup finely diced carrot
¼ cup finely diced celery
1 teaspoon minced garlic
17 ounces canned crabmeat, drained
¼ cup crème fraîche
¼ cup fresh parsley, chopped
¼ cup plus 2 tablespoons breadcrumbs, divided
1 tablespoon Dijon mustard
½ teaspoon paprika
¼ teaspoon cayenne pepper
1 lemon, juiced
Salt, to taste
Freshly ground black pepper, to taste
¾ cup grated Parmesan cheese
1 tablespoon honey

SPECIAL TOOLS
Six 6-ounce ramekins

Preheat the oven to 400°F.

Add the oil and butter to a medium sauté pan over medium heat. When the butter begins to foam, add the shallot, bell pepper, carrot, celery, and garlic. Cook until just tender but not browned, about 7 to 9 minutes. Remove from the heat and set aside to cool.

In a large bowl, mix together the crabmeat, crème fraîche, parsley, 2 tablespoons of the breadcrumbs, mustard, paprika, cayenne, lemon juice, salt, and pepper. Add the cooled vegetable mixture and mix thoroughly.

Fill each ramekin with the crab mixture. Place the ramekins on a rimmed baking sheet and bake for 15 to 17 minutes or until slightly brown across their tops.

While ramekins bake, make the topping. In a small bowl, mix the Parmesan cheese, the remaining ¼ cup of breadcrumbs, and honey until crumbs and cheese are evenly moistened.

Once the crab mixture is browned across the top, remove ramekins from the oven. Turn the broiler on high. Sprinkle the cheese mixture evenly across the top of each ramekin.

Return the ramekins to the oven and broil for 1 to 3 minutes until the tops are crisp and golden-brown. Watch carefully so they don't burn. Serve immediately. Leftovers can be covered and refrigerated for up to 2 days.

CHAPTER 4

Really BIG Snacks

Sometimes a big appetite calls for a big snack, and these are as big as they come! Some folks might consider these main meals, but Scooby and the gang don't like to limit themselves with labels. Sure, these recipes make bountiful breakfasts, large lunches, and daunting dinners, but we think they should be enjoyed any time of day — or night.

C.R.U.S.T. Sticky Situation

Yield: 4 servings
V

Some cases are bigger than Mystery Inc. can handle alone. When visiting the Center for Research and Understanding the Science of Toast (C.R.U.S.T.) in *Be Cool, Scooby-Doo!*, the gang joined superspy Jenny Vex on her mission to stop super-villains from threatening breakfast. Their sticky situation ended thanks to an explosion of jam . . . just like the one that bursts from this stuffed French toast!

JAM BUTTER
4 tablespoons salted butter, softened
1 tablespoon raspberry jam

CUSTARD
1 ½ cups whole milk
3 tablespoons powdered sugar
1 tablespoon vanilla extract
4 eggs

PEANUT BUTTER SYRUP
2 tablespoons peanut butter
3 tablespoons maple syrup
½ tablespoon unsalted butter

FRENCH TOAST
8 pieces sliced bread, soft buttermilk or white
½ cup smooth peanut butter, divided
¼ cup raspberry jam, divided
2 tablespoons unsalted butter, divided

To make the jam butter: In a small bowl or ramekin, blend the butter and jam together with a fork. Set aside until serving.

To make the custard: In a shallow dish, large enough to fit a slice of bread, whisk together the milk, powdered sugar, and vanilla. Add the eggs, one at a time, whisking after each addition, until the mixture is homogenized. Set aside.

To make the peanut butter syrup: In a microwave-safe pitcher or measuring cup, combine the peanut butter, maple syrup, and butter. Heat in the microwave for 30 seconds, and then stir until smooth.

To make the French toast: Working with two pieces of bread at a time, spread about 1 tablespoon of peanut butter onto each slice. Use the back of a teaspoon to make a shallow indent into the center of one piece of bread. Fill the indent with about ½ tablespoon of jam. Make a sandwich with the two prepared pieces of bread, pressing them together lightly to adhere.

In a medium skillet over medium-high heat, melt ½ tablespoon of butter. Once the butter begins to melt, dunk the sandwich in the egg custard, making sure to coat both sides. Letting the excess drip off, place the sandwich into the pan. Brown on each side for 3 to 4 minutes until golden-brown. Repeat with the remaining slices of bread. To serve, top with jam butter and drizzle with peanut butter syrup.

The French toast can be served immediately or kept warm on a plate in a 200°F oven.

Save Breakfast!

Yield: 4 servings
GF

When teaming up with Agent Jenny Vex to save breakfast, the gang learned that "Omelettes Are Forever." But even if a mission doesn't go as smoothly as hoped, and things get a little scrambled along the way, the final outcome can still be just as delicious. Case in point: This *eggs-ceptional* loaded scramble. It's truly a breakfast worth fighting for!

- 8 pieces thick-cut bacon, diced
- 2 tablespoons vegetable oil
- ½ white onion, diced
- 1 orange bell pepper, diced
- 1 pound frozen hash browns, shredded
- 1 ½ cups shredded cheddar cheese blend, divided
- 12 eggs
- ½ cup whole milk or half-and-half
- ½ teaspoon salt
- Freshly ground black pepper, to taste
- ½ cup sour cream, for garnish
- 4 green onions, finely chopped, white and light green parts, for garnish

In a large sauté pan over medium-high heat, cook the bacon until all the fat has been rendered and the bacon is crispy, about 7 to 10 minutes. Remove the bacon from the pan with a slotted spoon, transferring it to a paper towel–lined plate. When the bacon is cool enough to handle, crumble it into bite-sized pieces and set aside. Reserve 2 tablespoons of the bacon fat, discarding the rest. Remove from the heat and set aside.

Grease a rimmed baking sheet with the vegetable oil and preheat the sheet in the oven to 425°F.

Return the pan to the stove, over medium heat. When the bacon fat is melted and begins to shimmer, add the onion and bell pepper. Sauté until softened, about 5 to 7 minutes. Remove from the heat.

On the baking sheet, shape the potatoes into four equal portions. Use a spatula to flatten down each pile as you go.

Bake the hash browns for 20 minutes. Flip each pile over, and shape into a rough rectangle, flattening the hash browns as needed. Bake for another 10 minutes, flip again, and cover each pile in approximately ¼ cup of shredded cheese. Bake for another 5 minutes until the cheese is melted and bubbly. Turn off the oven but keep the hash browns inside to keep warm.

While the hash browns are baking, prepare the eggs. In a medium bowl, whisk the eggs, milk, salt, and pepper together. Return the sauté pan over medium heat, and mix the eggs and vegetables, stirring constantly to scramble. When the eggs are almost completely cooked, remove from the heat. Stir in the bacon and remaining ½ cup of cheese. Continue to stir until the cheese is melted.

To serve, place a portion of hash browns on a plate and cover with ¼ of the egg mixture. Garnish with a dollop of sour cream and sprinkle of green onions. Serve immediately with Bayou Pierre's Hot Sauce (page 13), if desired.

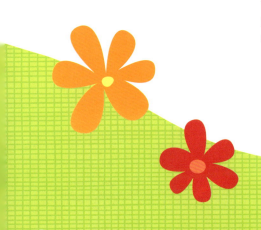

Ghost Pirate Stew

Yield: 6 servings
GF

When Shaggy and Scooby first cooked Ghost Pirate Stew in one of Mystery Inc.'s earliest cases, they were trying to trick the Ghost of Redbeard by throwing anything in the pot that they could find. That early version included a mixture of seawater and soap that left our dauntless duo burping bubbles. While this stew bears the same name, luckily, the recipe has been improved by fathoms!

SEAFOOD STOCK

- 3 leeks
- 1 pound shrimp
- 4 cups vegetable stock
- 1 cup water
- 1 tablespoon black peppercorns

STEW

- 1 tablespoon cornstarch
- 1 teaspoon kosher salt, divided
- ½ teaspoon freshly ground black pepper
- ½ pound squid rings and tentacles
- 2 tablespoons neutral oil
- 2 tablespoons unsalted butter
- Reserved white and light green parts of the leeks
- 1 shallot, thinly sliced
- ½ cup sweet vermouth
- 1 pound red potatoes, cut into bite-sized pieces
- 5 cups seafood stock, see note
- 2 bay leaves
- 2 tablespoons minced dill
- Zest 1 lemon
- 1 cup cream
- 1 pound clams, in their shells
- 1 pound cod, cut into bite-sized pieces
- Lemon wedges, optional

NOTE: You can take a shortcut with this recipe by buying good-quality seafood stock instead of preparing your own.

To make the seafood stock: Trim the rough outer leaves and the dark green ends off the leeks, rinse well, and cut into large chunks. Thinly slice the remaining light green and white parts. Cover and refrigerate until needed.

Leaving the tails on, peel and devein the shrimp. Reserve the peels. Cover and refrigerate the shrimp until needed. In a large pot, over medium-high heat, mix the vegetable stock, water, peppercorns, chunks of leeks, and shrimp peels. Bring to a boil, reduce to a simmer, and simmer for 20 to 30 minutes. Allow to cool for 10 to 15 minutes before straining. Discard the solids and reserve the stock. The stock can be made ahead of time and can be refrigerated in an airtight container for up to 1 day.

To make the stew: In a medium-sized bowl, mix together the cornstarch, ½ teaspoon of the salt, and black pepper. Pat the squid pieces dry with paper towels and add them to the bowl, tossing to thoroughly coat the squid in the mixture.

In a large Dutch oven, over medium-high heat, heat the oil. When the oil begins to shimmer, drop in the squid pieces along with any loose cornstarch mixture. Sauté until the squid is firm, and the mixture begins to brown and smell nutty, about 3 to 5 minutes.

Add the butter, reserved thinly sliced leeks, and shallot. Sauté until the leeks are softened and beginning to brown, about 5 to 7 minutes. Add the vermouth and deglaze the pan, cooking for about 3 minutes. Add the potatoes, seafood stock, remaining ½ teaspoon of salt, and the bay leaves. Bring the stew to a boil, reduce to a simmer, and cook for 10 to 15 minutes or until the potatoes are just fork-tender.

While the potatoes cook, combine the dill and lemon zest in a small bowl. When the potatoes are tender, add the cream and stir to combine. Mix in the clams, cod pieces, and reserved shrimp. Simmer until the clams open, the fish is opaque, and the shrimp is pink, about 5 minutes.

Serve in shallow bowls and top with a sprinkle of the dill mixture. Make sure guests have a discard bowl handy for clam shells and shrimp tails.

Pairs well with warm crusty bread. Leftovers can be stored in an airtight container for up to 1 day.

REALLY BIG SNACKS

Sinister Spaghetti

Yield: 8 servings
V

Who's got the beat? Luna, the drummer for the Hex Girls, does! Who's got the beets? We do! They're the secret ingredient in this blood red spaghetti sauce that the Hex Girls simmer up on their tour in *Scooby-Doo and Guess Who?* Add some Mozzarella Skulls (page 19) to the plate and this petrifying pasta instantly goes from filling to chilling!

Two 8.25-ounce cans sliced beets
2 tablespoons olive oil
1 tablespoon salted butter
4 large cloves garlic, minced
¼ cup salt-cured black olives, pitted
½ cup red wine
Two 15-ounce cans tomato sauce
One 6-ounce can tomato paste
One 14.5-ounce can diced tomatoes
8 ounces rainbow baby carrots
1 ½ pounds spaghetti noodles
Mozzarella Skulls (page 19), optional

Reserving the liquid, drain the beets and dice them. Set both aside. In a large pot or Dutch oven, over medium heat, add the olive oil and butter. When the butter foams, add the garlic and sauté until translucent, about 2 to 3 minutes. Add the beets, beet liquid, and olives. Continue to cook for another 2 to 3 minutes. Add the wine, stir to combine, and continue to cook for another 5 minutes.

Add the tomato sauce, tomato paste, and diced tomatoes. Stir to combine. Bring to a boil, then reduce to a simmer for 15 to 20 minutes. Stir frequently to prevent burning.

While the sauce is simmering, use a melon baller or paring knife to score knuckles into the carrots. Remove a bit from the end of each one creating the nail bed. See page 43 for more-detailed instructions. Once you have shaped all the carrot fingers, add them to the pot.

Cook the pasta according to package directions, drain, and add to the sauce. Serve immediately garnished with Mozzarella Skulls, if using. Leftovers can be stored in an airtight container, refrigerated, for up to 3 days.

REALLY BIG SNACKS

Rizza Rie with Cherry Sauce

Yield: Two 8-inch round pizzas

Shaggy says, "When things get scary, the scared get pizza. And when things get extra scary, we get extra-deep dish." He and Scooby-Doo love a piping hot pizza pie—or as Scooby says, a "rizza rie!" This one is inspired by a signature Shaggy Snack, a pizza pot pie with pepperoni, anchovies, and savory cherries. Its far-out flavors are sure to tickle the taste buds!

DOUGH
1 cup warm water
1 teaspoon granulated sugar
1 package active dry yeast, about 2 ¼ teaspoons
2 ½ cups bread flour
1 teaspoon kosher salt
5 tablespoons olive oil, divided

SAUCE
3 cups fresh cherries, stemmed and pitted
2 tablespoons olive oil
1 shallot, thinly sliced
4 to 6 anchovy filets, see note
2 tablespoons balsamic vinegar
Freshly ground black pepper, to taste
½ teaspoon salt
½ teaspoon pepper flakes
¼ cup fresh basil leaves

TOPPINGS
4 ounces uncured pepperoni
3 cups shredded mozzarella
1 cup grated Parmesan cheese
Extra anchovy filets, optional
Savory Double Dutch Chocolate Syrup (page 11), optional

SPECIAL TOOLS
Stand mixer fitted with a dough hook
Two 8-inch, 2-inch-deep cake pans
Offset spatula

To make the dough: In a small bowl or measuring cup, heat the water to between 110°F and 114°F. Stir in the sugar and sprinkle the yeast over the top, stir once more and set aside for 5 minutes.

In the bowl of a stand mixer, combine the flour, salt, and 1 tablespoon of the olive oil. Add the bloomed-yeast mixture and stir on low until a shaggy dough forms. Cover the bowl with a clean tea towel and allow it to rest for 10 minutes.

After 10 minutes, turn the mixer back to low and knead it for 5 to 10 minutes or until it starts to form a smooth ball. Oil a large bowl with a tablespoon of olive oil, place the dough in the bottom, cover tightly with plastic wrap, and allow to rise in a warm spot for 2 hours or until doubled in size. While the dough is rising, make the sauce.

To make the sauce: Roughly chop the cherries and add to a medium bowl along with any juices. Set aside. In a large sauté pan, over medium-high heat, combine the olive oil and sliced shallot. Sauté until the shallots are softened and begin to brown, about 3 to 5 minutes.

Add the anchovy and sauté another 1 to 2 minutes, breaking up the filets. Add the cherries, balsamic vinegar, black pepper, salt, and pepper flakes. Bring the mixture to a low boil. Reduce the heat to medium or medium-low and continue to simmer until the cherries begin to break down and the mixture turns jammy, 10 to 15 minutes. Be sure to stir frequently to prevent burning. When the sauce is done, remove from the heat. Chiffonade the basil leaves and stir into the sauce. Set aside.

To assemble the pizzas: Once the dough has risen, preheat the oven to 500°F. Grease the two pans with a tablespoon of olive oil each, making sure to go up the sides as well as the bottom. Split the dough between the two pans and let it rest for 5 minutes before gently stretching it to the edges of the pan. Drizzle half of the remaining tablespoon of olive oil over each pan. Use your fingers to press into the dough, creating dimples over the surface. Spread half of the cherry mixture over each pan and top each with half the slices of pepperoni.

In a medium bowl, mix the two cheeses together and then split between each pizza. Spread the cheese evenly, making sure it goes all the way to the edges.

Bake for 10 to 13 minutes, or until the cheese is starting to blacken at the edges and brown in the center. Remove from the oven and run an offset spatula around the edges to loosen. Let rest for 5 minutes before cutting into wedges and serving.

Stakeout? I'd Rather Have a Steak In!

Yield: 6 to 8 servings
GF

Sometimes solving a case requires long nights sitting in the Mystery Machine waiting and watching for clues. When it's time for a stakeout, this marinated sirloin will keep your crew going all night long. This recipe calls for a massive hunk of meat, so expect it to feed an entire van full of ghost hunters . . . or one very hungry Shaggy!

MARINADE

- 2 ½ to 3 pounds London broil, see note
- 1 ½ tablespoons salt
- 2 teaspoons freshly ground black pepper
- 4 cloves garlic, smashed and peeled
- 2 sprigs fresh rosemary, lightly crushed
- ¼ cup olive oil
- 2 tablespoons vegetable oil

SAUCE

- ½ cup sweet vermouth
- 1 tablespoon freshly ground black pepper
- 4 tablespoons unsalted butter

NOTE: London Broil, sometimes called top round, bottom round, or chuck steak, is a great choice for a less-expensive cut. It is lean and benefits from plenty of time in the marinade to boost its flavor and tenderness. This classic peppercorn sauce will work for your other favorite cuts as well.

To make the marinade: Poke the steak all over with a fork. In a large container with a tight-fitting lid, rub salt and pepper into the meat, making sure to get all sides. Add the garlic cloves, rosemary sprigs, and olive oil. Cover and refrigerate for at least 4 hours, turning once. You can also refrigerate for up to 24 hours but turn at least twice.

Thirty minutes before cooking, remove the steak from the refrigerator. Reserve two cloves of the garlic and one sprig of the rosemary from the marinade and discard the rest.

In a large cast-iron or stainless-steel skillet, over medium-high heat, heat the vegetable oil. When the oil begins to shimmer, add the steak. Cook on one side until well-browned, about 10 to 12 minutes. Use tongs to flip the steak and cook until well-browned or the internal temperature is 125°F (medium-rare) or 130°F (medium). The temperature will go up about 5°F while resting.

Once the meat is at the desired temperature, use the tongs to hold the steak while browning the edges, about 30 seconds each. Transfer the meat to a cutting board, loosely tent with foil, and let rest for 15 minutes.

To make the sauce: While the meat is resting, mince the reserved garlic cloves and rosemary. In the steak pan, over medium heat, sauté the garlic and rosemary, until the garlic is just becoming translucent, about 1 to 2 minutes.

Add the vermouth and use it to deglaze the pan, scraping up all the fond from the bottom of the pan. Add the black pepper and let the mixture come to a boil. Boil for 1 to 2 minutes before adding the butter and whisking to form a sauce. Once the sauce is emulsified, transfer it to a serving dish.

Thinly slice the steak against the grain and drizzle with a little of the sauce. Serve the rest of the sauce on the side.

Hex Fire Chili

Yield: 6 to 8 servings
V, V+*, GF

In the music world, there's no band hotter than the Hex Girls. And in the culinary world, there's no dish hotter than this spicy chili that the Hex Girls serve backstage at their concerts in *Scooby-Doo and Guess Who?* A few spoonfuls of this sizzling dish will burn up your mouth while the Girls are busy burning up the stage!

CHILI

2 tablespoons vegetable oil
1 large red onion, diced
2 jalapeños, seeded and diced
One 14 ½-ounce can diced tomatoes
1 teaspoon salt
½ teaspoon cayenne pepper
2 chipotle peppers in adobo sauce, diced, see note
One 15-ounce can pinto beans
One 15-ounce can black beans
One 15-ounce can red kidney beans
One 15-ounce can tomato sauce
½ teaspoon ground cumin
½ teaspoon Mexican oregano

CREMA

½ bunch cilantro, tough bottom stems removed
1 ripe avocado
¾ teaspoon salt
½ lime, juiced, about 1 ½ tablespoons
½ cup sour cream

SPECIAL TOOL

Blender or food processor

To make the chili: In a large pot, preferably a Dutch oven, over medium-high, heat the oil until it begins to shimmer. Add the red onion and the jalapeño and sauté, stirring continuously, until the onions are translucent and beginning to brown.

Add the diced tomatoes, salt, and cayenne pepper, stir to combine. Allow to cook 5 to 10 minutes until the tomatoes are jammy, stirring only occasionally. Once most of the liquid has evaporated, add the chipotle peppers and continue to cook another 2 to 3 minutes.

With their liquid, add the pinto beans, black beans, and red kidney beans. Stir to combine and sauté for 2 to 3 minutes.

Add the tomato sauce, cumin, and oregano, stir to combine. Bring to a gentle boil and then reduce to a simmer. Simmer for 30 to 45 minutes, until the mixture is slightly thickened.

To make the crema: Add the cilantro, avocado, salt, lime juice, and sour cream to a blender or food processor. Blend until completely smooth, stopping to scrape down the bowl once. Transfer to a serving dish.

To serve, ladle the chili into bowls and top with a dollop of crema (about 2 tablespoons). Serve immediately. Leftovers of the chili and crema can be stored in separate, airtight containers in the refrigerator for up to 3 days.

NOTE: Chipotle peppers in adobo sauce add a smokey heat. Where there's smoke, there's fire and we consider this to be a two-alarm level of heat. Want to ratchet up the heat? Add more chipotle peppers, one for each flame. Let the chili simmer for at least 20 minutes, then taste for spice level. If desired, add 1 chipotle pepper at a time, simmer for 10 minutes, and check the spice level between each addition.

*This recipe can be made vegan by using a plant-based sour cream or plant-based plain yogurt.

REALLY BIG SNACKS

Hot Dog Tacos with All the Trimmings

Yield: 8 tacos
GF*

There's only one dog that Shaggy loves almost as much as Scooby-Doo: A hot dog! (Especially the kind with all the trimmings from the Funland amusement park!) How do you make the perfect snack even better? Cross a hot dog and a taco! This pairing is so palate-pleasing that our dauntless duo eventually made it a featured food at their own amusement park, Shaggy and Scooby World!

CORN SALSA

2 ears corn
1 teaspoon vegetable oil
1 avocado
1 lime, juiced
1 cup cherry tomatoes, quartered
½ teaspoon salt

TACOS

8 hot dogs
½ onion, diced
½ bunch cilantro, leaves picked and roughly chopped
1 cup shredded pepper jack or jack cheese
8 hard taco shells, see note
1 cup Savory Double Dutch Chocolate Syrup (page 11)
½ cups Sweet Cherry Relish (page 12), optional

SPECIAL TOOL

1 wooden skewer

NOTE: Hard-shell tacos add a fun crunch to this dish but corn tortillas prepared in your favorite way will work too. *Make sure to choose all-corn flour tortillas to keep this dish gluten free. Plant-based hot dogs can be used to make this dish vegetarian.

To make the corn salsa: Preheat the oven to 450°F.

Shuck the corn and coat it with the oil. Place on a rimmed baking sheet and roast the corn for 10 to 12 minutes, or until very brown in some spots and fork-tender. Halfway through cooking, shake the corn back and forth to turn it over. Remove from the oven and allow to cool. Lower the oven temperature to 400°F and keep the baking sheet standing by.

While the corn is cooling, dice the avocado and combine it in a medium-sized bowl with the lime juice, tomatoes, and salt. Once the corn is cool enough to handle, stand it on end and use a knife to cut the kernels away from the cob. Add the corn to the bowl and stir to combine. Set aside until needed for serving.

To make the tacos: Run a wooden skewer through a hot dog from end to end, as straight as possible. With the skewer still in the hot dog, use a paring knife to slice the hot dog. Holding the knife at a slight angle, slowly roll the hot dog as you gently make a spiral cut from end to end. The skewer will prevent you from cutting all the way through. Gently push the hot dog off the skewer, place it on the baking sheet, and repeat with the remaining dogs. Once you have spiralized all the hot dogs, bake them for 10 to 13 minutes or until brown and crispy. Transfer them to a serving plate.

While the hot dogs are baking, combine the diced onion and cilantro in a medium-sized bowl, and warm up the Savory Double Dutch Chocolate Syrup in a microwave-safe bowl.

To serve, set up all the components for guests as a taco bar or fill each taco shell with corn salsa, top with a hot dog, cheese, onion, cilantro, and Savory Double Dutch Chocolate Syrup and Sweet Cherry Relish, if using. Serve immediately; leftovers can be stored in the refrigerator in airtight containers for up to 3 days.

REALLY BIG SNACKS

Jeepers! It's the Creeper Dog

Yield: 6 corn dogs
V*, GF

One of Mystery Inc.'s most memorable cases pitted them against the massive mutant called The Creeper. He may have just been bank president Mr. Carswell in disguise, but his villainous visage has haunted the gang for years. Whenever the memory of his freakish facade triggers a bout of stress-eating, this Creeper-themed corn dog succeeds at curbing their appetites and fears.

TOPPINGS

¼ cup smooth peanut butter
¼ teaspoon salt
¼ teaspoon chile powder
⅛ teaspoon cayenne pepper, optional
1 teaspoon black cocoa powder
15 to 20 blue-corn chips, ground
1 thin green onion

CORN DOGS

6 precooked sausages or hot dogs, see note
1 cup cornmeal
½ cup corn flour
½ cup mochiko flour
2 teaspoons baking powder
½ teaspoon baking soda
1 teaspoon granulated sugar
1 teaspoon salt
½ teaspoon freshly ground black pepper
1 teaspoon garlic powder
2 teaspoons spirulina
2 quarts frying oil, such as vegetable, peanut, canola, or safflower
¾ cup whole milk
¼ cup apple cider vinegar
2 eggs

SPECIAL TOOLS

Food processor or spice grinder
6 long wooden skewers
Candy thermometer
Offset spatula
Piping bag

NOTE: *These can be made with plant-based sausages for a vegetarian option.

To prepare the toppings: In a small bowl, combine the peanut butter, salt, chile powder, cayenne, and black cocoa powder. Stir until smooth. Transfer to a pastry bag and refrigerate until needed.

Using a food processor or spice grinder, process the corn chips until they are a uniform sandy consistency. Place in a small bowl and set aside. Thinly slice the green onion, white parts only, cover and refrigerate until needed.

To make the corn dogs: In a medium skillet, over medium-high heat, brown the sausages on all sides, about 3 to 5 minutes. Remove to a paper towel–lined plate and set aside.

In a medium bowl, mix together the cornmeal, corn flour, mochiko, baking powder, baking soda, granulated sugar, salt, pepper, garlic powder, and spirulina. Whisk until thoroughly combined and set aside. Lengthwise, pierce the sausage with a skewer, keeping the stick as straight as possible. Make sure the skewers are inserted almost the entire length of each sausage. Repeat for all sausages.

Heat the frying oil in either a deep fryer or a large Dutch oven. Using a candy thermometer, heat the oil to around 350°F. Preheat the oven to 250°F and line a baking sheet with parchment paper. See Fry Station Safety Tips, page 139.

As the oil gets close to 300°F, mix the milk, vinegar, and eggs together in a medium bowl. Add this to the dry mixture and stir until all the dry ingredients have been incorporated. When the temperature reaches 350°F, fill a tall glass with batter. Holding the sausage by the end of the stick, dip it into the batter. You can also use a small offset spatula to spread the batter onto the sausages. Then dip into the frying oil. Holding onto the stick, slowly spin the corn dog until it's brown on all sides, about 2 to 3 minutes.

Remove the corn dog from the oil and place it on the prepared baking sheet. Place the baking sheet in the oven and repeat the process with the remaining sausages.

When all the sausages have been fried and baked for a minimum of 3 minutes, remove the baking sheet from the oven and decorate. Pipe the spicy peanut butter onto the top of the corn dog and press it into the corn chips. Pipe on the mouth and scar. Pipe small dots for the eyes to glue on the green onion slices and then pipe a small dot in the center of each for the pupil. Serve immediately with the spicy mustard from the Spicy Funky Fritters (page 42), your favorite mustard, or ketchup. Leftovers can be stored in an airtight container in the refrigerator for up to 3 days.

Mini Burgers in a Pile

Yield: 16 burgers

What's better than a perfectly cooked hamburger? How about a whole pile of them?! These bite-sized burgers are perfect for sharing, but you could also just devour a stack of them solo, Scooby-style! Serve them up on a fancy platter or on the Mystery Machine's hubcap—they'll taste great either way!

BUNS

Two 11-ounce refrigerated bread dough canisters or around 22 ounces frozen parker roll or bread dough

4 tablespoons salted butter, softened, divided

1 tablespoon sesame seeds, toasted

BURGERS

2 ½ pounds ground beef

2 ½ teaspoons salt

Freshly ground black pepper, to taste

1 yellow onion, diced

8 pieces American cheese, cut into quarters

⅓ cup Sweet Cherry Relish (page 12)

16 Roma tomato slices, optional

To make the buns: Preheat the oven to 350°F and grease two rimmed baking sheets with about 1 tablespoon of the butter.

Remove the bread logs from their packaging and cut each log into eight equal pieces. Gently knead each piece to form a circle, about 3 inches across. Place the dough pieces on the baking sheet about 2 inches apart. Use a sharp knife to score an X across the top of each bun.

Melt the remaining butter and use a pastry brush to brush each bun. Sprinkle with sesame seeds and bake for 15 to 18 minutes or until golden-brown. Remove from the oven and cool on sheets. Cut each bun in half with a serrated knife and set aside until serving.

To make the patties: Preheat the oven to 425°F and place one of the baking sheets inside. Cover the bottom of the second baking sheet in foil and set aside.

Combine the beef with salt and pepper and divide into sixteen equal balls. When the oven reaches the desired temperature, remove the baking sheet to a heat-proof surface. Place the meatballs on the hot baking sheet, leaving about 2 inches of space in between. Use the second baking sheet to smash the burgers into patties. Cover the top of each patty with onions and return to the oven. Bake for 10 to 12 minutes or until a meat thermometer reads 145°F. Remove from the oven once more and place two cheese quarters on each patty. Return to the oven for 1 to 2 minutes more, or until the cheese is melted.

To serve, spread about a teaspoon of Sweet Cherry Relish onto each bun bottom, top with a patty, a tomato slice, if using, and top bun. Pile high on a platter and serve with Finger (and Toe) Fries (page 43).

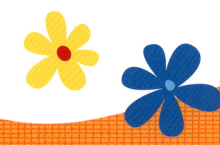

REALLY BIG SNACKS

CHAPTER 5

Sandwich Snacks

After extensive research, Shaggy and Scooby have determined that the very best type of snack is the kind served between two slices of bread. Velma has serious questions about the methods used to determine that data. But even she can't deny that her pals were really on a roll when they came up with this spectacular selection of sandwiches!

Goth Bites

Yield: 24 sandwiches
V

One of the things fans love about the Hex Girls is that each of the spine-chilling songstresses brings their own distinct flavor to the band's sound. The same goes for these small sandwiches, with raspberry-rose jam representing Thorn, spinach pesto for Dusk, and a purple carrot and blackberry chèvre filling for Luna. Now that's good taste in music!

THORN'S RASPBERRY-ROSE SANDWICH

1 cup fresh or frozen raspberries
1 cup granulated sugar
1 teaspoon rose water
½ chocolate hazelnut spread
8 pieces dark bread
16 pine nuts

NOTE: The fillings can be made up to a day ahead and stored in airtight containers in the refrigerator until needed. The lip pieces can be precut up to a day ahead and stored in an airtight container or plastic bag as you would normally store bread. Assembly should be done as close to serving as possible so that the sandwiches don't dry out. Save the bread scraps to make bread crumbs or croutons. If your bread slices are on the small size, cut one full lip and then use the cutter to cut just the top lip from the remaining part of the slice.

To make Thorn's raspberry-rose sandwich: Put a small plate in the freezer while preparing the jam.

In a medium saucepan over medium-high heat, combine the raspberries and sugar, stirring constantly. Once the sugar is dissolved, let the mixture come to a boil and cook for 5 to 7 minutes. Stir regularly to prevent burning and bubbling over.

After 7 minutes, remove from the heat and put a teaspoon of jam on the plate in the freezer. Set a timer for 2 minutes before testing the jam. Run a finger through the jam. If it holds the path and feels firm, the jam is ready. If it's easy to pull your finger through or easy to move the jam, return the pot to the stove. Bring the jam back to a boil and cook for an additional 5 minutes, stirring frequently. Test again. When the jam is ready, strain through a fine-mesh strainer, discarding the seeds. Stir in the rose water and decant into a heat-proof jar. Refrigerate until completely cool.

To assemble the sandwich, cut two lips from each piece of bread. Spread about 1 tablespoon of the chocolate hazelnut onto eight lips. Place the eight pieces of bread onto a plate or small cutting board, and chill for 15 minutes.

Remove from the refrigerator and spread a thin layer of jam over each lip. With the remaining eight lips, use kitchen shears or a sharp knife and trim the bottom lip off. Place the top lip on the jam, creating the completed sandwich. Insert two pine nut fangs into the seam between the top lip and the filling.

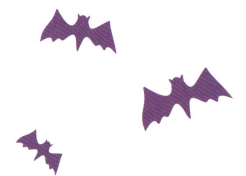

RECIPE CONTINUES ON PAGE 74

72

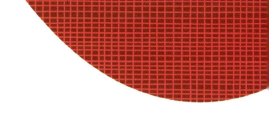

LUNA'S BLACKBERRY-CARROT SANDWICH

4 purple carrots, cut into 1-inch chunks

1 teaspoon olive oil

½ cup blackberries

1 teaspoon balsamic vinegar glaze

½ teaspoon salt

Freshly ground black pepper, to taste

8 pieces dark bread

4 ounces chèvre, divided

16 pine nuts

DUSK'S PESTO SANDWICHES

1 cup baby spinach leaves

1 cup basil leaves

¼ cup pepitas

2 teaspoons lemon juice

¼ teaspoon salt

½ teaspoon freshly ground black pepper

3 tablespoons olive oil

2 tablespoons grated Parmesan cheese

8 pieces dark bread

4 ounces whipped cream cheese

16 pine nuts

SPECIAL TOOLS

Fine-mesh strainer

Blender or food processor

4 ½-inch lip cookie cutters

To make Luna's blackberry-carrot sandwich: Preheat the oven to 375°F.

Place the carrots on a rimmed baking sheet, toss with the olive oil, and bake for 15 to 20 minutes or until fork-tender. Cool for 5 minutes.

Place the carrots in a blender or a food processor with the blackberries and balsamic glaze. Process until mostly smooth and a thick paste. Add salt and pepper, then process again briefly to combine. Store in an airtight container in the refrigerator until ready to use.

To assemble the sandwich, cut two lips from each piece of bread and spread about a tablespoon of chèvre onto eight pieces. Generously spread the blackberry-carrot mixture over the cheese. With the remaining eight lips, use kitchen shears or a sharp knife and trim the bottom lip off. Place the top lip on the jam, creating the completed sandwich. Insert two pine nut fangs into the seam between the top lip and the filling.

To make Dusk's pesto sandwiches: In the bowl of a food processor, or strong blender, combine the spinach, basil, pepitas, lemon juice, salt, and pepper. Blend on high to finely chop the leaves. Add the olive oil and blend again to create a smooth paste. Add the Parmesan and pulse briefly to combine. Store in an airtight container and refrigerate until needed.

To assemble the sandwich, cut two lips from each piece of bread and spread about a tablespoon of whipped cream cheese onto eight pieces. Generously spread the pesto over the cheese. With the remaining eight lips, use kitchen shears or a sharp knife and trim the bottom lip off. Place the top lip on the jam, creating the completed sandwich. Insert two pine nut fangs into the seam between the top lip and the filling.

Serve the sandwiches immediately or store in a single layer in an airtight container in the refrigerator for up to 3 hours.

Super-Duper Hero Sandwich

Yield: 4 servings

Shaggy and Scooby are usually Mystery Inc.'s resident sandwich artists, but the gang's other members have been known to build an impressive snack stack themselves. Fred and Daphne piled this sky-high sub with meats, cheeses, and spreads to entice Scooby into action. This high-stacked hero could inspire even the most cowardly canine into playing a hero of a different kind!

½ red onion, thinly sliced

1 ½ tablespoons red wine vinegar

½ teaspoon salt

1 ½ teaspoons dried oregano

½ teaspoon dried minced garlic

Freshly ground black pepper, to taste

¼ cup mayonnaise

2 tablespoons yellow mustard

½ teaspoon onion powder

¼ teaspoon paprika

One 16-ounce bread Italian loaf, about 14 inches in length

½ small head iceberg lettuce, thinly sliced

2 tablespoons olive oil

6 slices provolone, about 6 ounces

½ cup banana pepper rings, mild or hot

8 ounces sliced peppered deli turkey

3 ounces genoa salami

3 ounces mortadella

3 ounces calabrese salami

Tomato, halved and thinly sliced, optional

4 pimento olives

½ cup pepperoncini peppers

SPECIAL TOOLS

Long cutting board

4 sandwich picks

In a medium bowl, mix together the red onion, vinegar, salt, oregano, garlic, and black pepper. Set aside.

In a small bowl, combine the mayonnaise, mustard, onion powder, and paprika. Cover and refrigerate until needed.

Cut the loaf of bread in half, lengthwise. Using the top slice, pull out some of the bread from the center, creating a trench about 1 inch deep and the length of the bread.

Add the lettuce and olive oil to the onions and toss to combine and coat everything in the dressing.

Place the bottom piece of bread on the cutting board and spread the mayonnaise mixture from end to end. Layer on the cheese slices, covering the entire bottom and overlapping as needed. Cover the cheese with the banana peppers. Add about half the turkey slices, folding as necessary to create an even layer. Layer on all of the genoa salami, followed by the mortadella and the calabrese, pressing gently between each layer to keep the ingredients as level as possible. Layer on the remaining turkey. Cover in tomato slices, if using.

> **Tip:** It is helpful to have all the cheese and meats measured out and laid out on a large plate or tray.

Fill the trench in the top piece of bread with the lettuce-and-onion mixture, line the piece up with the assembled bottom, and carefully flip the top onto the bottom. Press down on the bread from end to end to level out the sandwich. Thread an olive onto each sandwich pick and secure the sandwich by placing the picks along the top, creating four sections.

To serve, place the pepperoncini peppers on one end of the board. Cut the sandwich into four equal sections and serve immediately. Leftovers can be stored in an airtight container for up to 24 hours.

SANDWICH SNACKS

Triple-Decker Veggie Club

Yield: 4 sandwiches
V, V+*, GF*

The best way to solve a mystery is to get someone to spill their secrets. When no one's talking, whip up one of these vegetarian delights—with meaty mushrooms, avocado spread, and Pickled Vampire Wings (page 30)—to loosen their lips. Because you know what they say about loose lips, right? "They're great for fitting around a Triple-Decker Veggie Club!" according to Shaggy in *What's New, Scooby-Doo?*

AVOCADO SPREAD
1 lime, juiced, about 2 tablespoons
2 avocados, pitted, peeled, and cubed
¾ teaspoon salt
½ teaspoon garlic powder
½ teaspoon ground mustard
2 tablespoons olive oil

MUSHROOMS
4 portobello mushrooms
4 tablespoons olive oil, divided
4 tablespoons salted butter, divided
1 teaspoon salt, divided
Freshly ground black pepper, to taste

SANDWICHES
12 slices sliced sourdough or buttermilk bread, divided
2 cups Pickled Vampire Wings (page 30)
8 slices tomato, divided
8 slices pepper jack cheese, divided
2 cups baby spinach leaves, divided

SPECIAL TOOLS
Blender or food processor
8 cocktail picks or long toothpicks

To make the avocado spread: In a blender or a food processor, mix the lime juice, avocado, salt, garlic powder, and mustard. Blend on high until very smooth, scraping down the mixture as necessary. Once smooth, add the olive oil and blend until the mixture is the consistency of mayonnaise, about 30 seconds. Decant to a small bowl and set aside.

To make the mushrooms: Slice the mushrooms into ¼-inch-thick slices. In a large skillet over medium-high heat, warm 2 tablespoons of the oil and 2 tablespoons of the butter. When the butter begins to foam, tilt the pan to spread out the mixture and then add about ½ of the mushrooms in a single layer. Cook for 2 to 3 minutes or until well-browned before turning over and cooking on the other side. Once this batch is well-browned and tender, sprinkle with ½ teaspoon of the salt and black pepper. Stir to coat and cook for about 1 minute more. Transfer to a plate and repeat with the second half of the mushrooms.

To assemble the sandwiches: Toast three pieces of bread per sandwich. Spread about 2 tablespoons of avocado spread on one slice, cover the spread with six to eight slices of mushroom, two pieces of cheese, and about ¼ cup of Pickled Vampire Wings.

Top with the second slice of bread. Spread about 2 tablespoons more of the avocado and top with two slices of tomato, another ¼ cup of Pickled Vampire Wings, and about ½ cup of spinach leaves. Top with the third slice of bread. Stick a cocktail pick into two opposite corners and cut the sandwich in half on an angle, creating two triangles. Serve immediately.

Repeat the steps to make the remaining sandwiches.

NOTE: Refrigerate any leftover spread in an airtight container for up to 2 days.
*This can be made vegan by using a plant-based cheese and gluten free by using your favorite gluten-free bread.

SANDWICH SNACKS

Ham Sandwich (to Calm My Nerves)

Yield: 1 sandwich

Chasing ghosts and catching criminals can really put a teen (and their dog) on edge! When the tension rises, Shaggy insists that there's nothing better to calm the nerves—and the stomach—than a nice, big ham sandwich with mustard. It may seem simple, but usually the best solutions are! Now if only solving every case was this easy . . .

MUSTARD SAUCE
2 tablespoons fig jam or Sweet Cherry Relish (page 12)
1 tablespoon balsamic vinegar
2 tablespoons stone-ground mustard
¼ teaspoon ground white pepper
¼ teaspoon freshly ground black pepper

SANDWICH
2 slices sourdough bread
1 tablespoon unsalted butter, divided
3 ounces Brie cheese, softened, divided
1 tablespoon mustard sauce, divided
3 slices deli ham, about 2 ½ ounces
3 slices prosciutto, about 1 ¼ ounces
¼ baby arugula leaves

To make the mustard sauce: In a small bowl, combine the jam and balsamic vinegar until it is combined. Stir in the mustard, white pepper, and black pepper and mix until incorporated. Set aside or refrigerate in an airtight container if not using right away.

To make the sandwich: Toast the bread until crispy and golden-brown. Spread the butter on one side of both pieces of bread. Slice the Brie, split it evenly between the slices of bread, and spread it out well. Spoon about ½ tablespoon of mustard sauce onto the Brie, on each slice. On one piece of the bread, layer the ham and prosciutto, alternating between the two. Cover the other piece of bread with the arugula leaves. Place the two halves of the sandwich together, slice in half, and serve.

NOTE: You should have enough sauce for four sandwiches.

SANDWICH SNACKS 81

Jaw-Stretcher Special

Yield: 4 sandwiches

The jaw-stretcher special has had many incarnations over the years. The name has been used to describe a number of sandwiches piled so high, or stuffed so full, that they push Shaggy and Scooby's mandibular muscles to the max. This twist on the classic concept adds an Italian flare, with meatballs, tomato sauce, mozzarella, and plenty of Parmesan!

2 Italian loaves or other soft loaves, approximately 14 inches long

¼ cup milk of choice

1 tablespoon dried minced garlic

1 teaspoon salt

2 tablespoons dried parsley

1 cup finely grated Pecorino Romano, plus more for serving

1 egg

1 pound ground beef

1 pound spicy Italian sausage, bulk or removed from casings

2 tablespoons vegetable oil

3 large cloves garlic, minced

1 tablespoon dried oregano

1 tablespoon balsamic vinegar

One 14.5-ounce can diced tomatoes

One 15-ounce can tomato sauce

1 cup shredded mozzarella, divided

Savory Double Dutch Chocolate Syrup (page 11), optional*

NOTE: Wrap up the rolls ⅔ of the way in foil before putting them in the oven. The foil cools quickly and will make them easier to handle and serve. Alternatively, you can wrap each roll in parchment when it comes out of the oven and stand it up in a small, galvanized bucket or heavy-bottomed glass.

*Add Savory Double Dutch Chocolate Syrup to top this sandwich just like Shaggy would!

Cut the loaves in half to create four small loaves. Working from the cut end, remove the majority of the soft interior. Wrap the hollowed loaves in their original packaging or plastic wrap and set them aside. Crumble the removed interior into small pieces. Measure out 2 loosely packed cups and put into a large bowl. Save the remainder of the bread crumbs for another purpose or discard.

To a medium bowl, add the milk, minced garlic, salt, and parsley. Let rest for 5 minutes before adding the cheese, egg, ground beef, and Italian sausage. Thoroughly combine the meat with your hands into a homogeneous mixture. Form into tight meatballs, approximately 3 ½ ounces each, twelve portions.

In a large ovenproof skillet, over medium-high heat, heat the vegetable oil until it begins to shimmer and spreads over the surface of the pan. Add the meatballs in a single layer and brown on all sides, about 3 to 5 minutes per side. Once the meatballs are brown, remove them to a paper towel–lined plate or rimmed baking sheet.

Add the garlic and the oregano to the pan and sauté until the garlic softens and it begins to brown, about 2 to 3 minutes. Add the balsamic vinegar and cook 1 minute more. Add the diced tomatoes, bring to a simmer, and cook until most of the liquid has been reduced and the mixture is jammy, about 7 to 10 minutes. Add the tomato sauce and stir to combine, cooking for 2 to 3 minutes.

In a single layer, add the meatballs to the sauce. Use a large spoon to ladle some sauce over the meatballs. Cover the pan with a lid and cook for 10 to 15 minutes or until the internal temperature of the meatballs reaches 165°F.

Toward the end of the meatball cooking time, preheat your oven to 375°F. Toast the rolls on a rimmed baking sheet for 7 to 10 minutes.

Ladle a bit of sauce into the bottom of each roll, about 2 tablespoons. Place one meatball in the sandwich and sprinkle about a tablespoon of mozzarella over it. Repeat these steps until each roll has three meatballs in it. Sprinkle with extra Pecorino Romano and serve immediately.

Hot Pepper Po' Boy

Yield: 4 sandwiches

When Mystery Inc. road-tripped down to the Big Easy to search for real ghosts, Shaggy and Scooby didn't miss a chance to eat one of the famous po' boy sandwiches from Pierre's Poor Boys, home of "The Biggest Poor Boys in New Orleans." This spicy sammie really turns up the heat. And like Shaggy says, "mo' hotter, mo' better!"

RELISH
8 ounces sweet chile peppers, stemmed

2 or 3 spicy peppers such as jalapeño, cayenne, or serrano

4 cloves garlic, minced

1 tablespoon salted butter

½ teaspoon kosher salt

⅓ cup apple cider vinegar

½ cup granulated sugar

2 tablespoons molasses

SHRIMP SANDWICHES
16 medium shrimp

2 teaspoons all-purpose flour

½ teaspoon kosher salt

1 teaspoon smoked paprika

½ teaspoon cayenne pepper

Freshly ground black pepper, to taste

4 tablespoons salted butter, divided

4 po' boy rolls

2 cups shredded iceberg lettuce, divided

½ small red onion, finely sliced, optional

16 slices tomato, optional

SPECIAL TOOL
Food processor

To make the relish: Cut the chile peppers into 2- to 3-inch pieces. Add the pieces to the bowl of a food processor and pulse two or three times until they are chopped down into relish-sized bits.

In a large sauté pan over medium-high heat, melt the butter, and add the chopped peppers, minced garlic, and salt. Stir constantly until the peppers are softened. Cook for 5 to 10 minutes.

Add the apple cider vinegar, sugar, and molasses. Stir to combine and bring the mixture to a boil. Reduce to medium-low and continue to simmer for 10 to 15 minutes or until the liquid has reduced and the mixture is jammy. Remove from the heat, transfer to a heat-proof container, and allow to cool completely. When cool, cover the mixture and refrigerate. The relish can be kept in the refrigerator for up to 1 week.

To make the shrimp and assemble the sandwiches: Peel, devein, and remove the tails of the shrimp. In a medium bowl, toss the flour, salt, paprika, cayenne, and black pepper together. Add the shrimp and toss them in the spice mixture until well coated.

Heat a large skillet over medium-high heat. Split the rolls, leaving them connected on one side, and butter both halves of each roll. Working with two rolls at a time, press the rolls, cut-side down, into the hot pan and toast 3 to 5 minutes until browned. Remove rolls from the pan and set aside. Repeat with the other two rolls.

Once the rolls have been browned, add the oil to the pan and heat for about 1 minute or until it begins to shimmer. Add the shrimp all at once. Shake the pan or use tongs to brown the shrimp on all sides, 2 to 3 minutes. Transfer the shrimp to a plate.

To build each sandwich, place a roll on a plate or in a sandwich basket and spread both halves of the roll with about a tablespoon of relish. Pile about ½ cup of shredded lettuce on the bottom half of the roll, top with sliced red onion, and four shrimp. If using, place the tomato slices on the top half of the roll and gently close the sandwich. Repeat until all the sandwiches have been assembled. Serve immediately. Any extra relish can be kept in an airtight container in the refrigerator for up to 1 week.

SANDWICH SNACKS

CHAPTER 6

Liquid Snacks

When you're on the hunt for fiends and foes, it's important to stay hydrated. Especially if you've been scarfing down salty and savory snacks along the way! Some of these bizarre beverages may not look safe to swig, but we assure you that these bewitching brews won't have any ill effects—other than making you want to drink a few more glasses!

Scooby Shake (and Shiver)

Yield: 2 shakes
V, GF*

When things get scary, Scooby-Doo has been known to freak out! Maybe that's why he goes crazy for this "freakshake"—a milkshake that packs in as many decadent dessert flavors as possible. With peanut butter ice cream, mini peanut butter cups, chocolate syrup, whipped cream, and pretzel rod tail, this shake is like a Scooby Snack, but in liquid form!

8 mini peanut butter cups, divided
2 full-sized peanut butter cups
5 tablespoons Sweet Double Dutch Chocolate Syrup (page 11), divided
4 large pretzel rods, divided
¾ cup heavy whipping cream
½ cup milk of choice
½ cup smooth peanut butter
4 cups vanilla ice cream

SPECIAL TOOLS
2 tall smooth glasses
Whipped cream canister, see note
Blender

Heat a microwave-safe plate in the microwave for 30 seconds and remove. Press the mini peanut butter cups to the plate, alternating between the tops and bottoms, melting them slightly. Press four mini cups onto the inside of each glass to create Scooby's spots. Cut each of the full-sized peanut butter cups in half and set aside with the glasses.

Fill a whipped cream canister with the heavy cream and 1 tablespoon of the chocolate syrup. Refrigerate until needed. Crush two of the pretzels and set aside in a small bowl.

In a large blender, mix the milk, peanut butter, and ice cream. Blend until smooth.

Carefully pour 2 tablespoons of the remaining chocolate syrup into each glass, being careful not to splash the sides. Pour the shake mixture between the two glasses. Add a whole pretzel rod to each glass and top with a generous portion of whipped cream. Place two halves of full-sized peanut cups, as ears, onto each glass. Garnish with crushed pretzel; serve immediately with a long spoon and straw.

NOTE: If you don't have a whipped cream canister, place the cream in a chilled, medium-sized bowl, add 1 tablespoon of chocolate syrup, and whisk on high with a hand mixer until stiff peaks form. Cover and refrigerate until needed.

Zoinks! It's a Shaggy Shake

Yield: 4 shakes
GF

We all know Shaggy loves outrageous flavor combinations in his food, so why should his beverages be any different? This classic chocolate milkshake has been completely Shaggified with tons of tasty toppings, like maple whipped cream, crumbled waffle cone, and candied bacon. This decadent drink is as bold as it is cold, and it goes perfect alongside any super-stacked sandwich!

CANDIED BACON

Cooking spray

8 slices bacon

2 tablespoons brown sugar

Pinch, ⅛ teaspoon or less, cayenne pepper

1 teaspoon cinnamon

1 teaspoon dark cocoa powder

1 teaspoon maple syrup

MILKSHAKE

1 cup heavy whipping cream

2 tablespoons maple syrup

8 large scoops ice cream, about 1 quart, divided

2 ½ cups whole milk, divided

½ cup Sweet Double Dutch Chocolate Syrup (page 11)

2 sugar cones, crumbled, divided

SPECIAL TOOLS

Rimmed baking sheet fitted with rack

Whipped cream canister or hand mixer fitted with a whisk attachment

Blender

To make the candied bacon: Spray the baking sheet and rack with cooking spray. Place parchment paper over the rack and use paring knife to poke holes throughout the surface. Preheat the oven to 375°F.

In a small bowl, mix together the brown sugar, cayenne, cinnamon, dark cocoa powder, and maple syrup. Pour the mixture out on a plate. Press the pieces of bacon into the spice mixture. Make sure pieces are covered on both sides and lay them out on the parchment paper without touching or overlapping.

Bake for 20 to 25 minutes or until dark and crisp. Completely cool on the rack. If not using right away, seal in an airtight container between layers of parchment.

To make the milkshake: Using a whipped cream canister or a hand mixer and a large bowl, whip the cream. Add in the maple syrup and whip until stiff peaks form.

For each milkshake, combine two large scoops of ice cream, one piece of bacon, and ½ cup plus 2 tablespoons of milk in a blender. Blend on high until desired consistency.

> **Tip:** Depending on the size of your blender, you may want to work in batches.

Using 2 tablespoons of chocolate syrup, coat or lace the inside of each glasse. Swirl around to ensure the inside is coated well. Split the milkshake between the glasses. Top with a large dollop of whipped cream and crumbled sugar cone. Garnish with one slice of bacon. Serve immediately.

LIQUID SNACKS

Looks Like We Got Ourselves a Protein Shake

Yield: 1 serving
V, V+, GF

Sometimes the members of Mystery Inc. complain that their leader, Fred Jones, can be a bit too vanilla—as in *boring*! But since when was vanilla a bad thing? Other flavors come and go, but you can always depend on vanilla to be there when you need it. Just like Fred. So this vanilla protein shake is the perfect tribute!

1 ripe banana, divided
8 ounces rice milk
1 serving vanilla plant-based protein powder, see note
¼ cup blueberries
2 tablespoons freshly squeezed orange juice
½ teaspoon blue spirulina powder
1 orange slice, for garnish

SPECIAL TOOLS
Blender
Tall, chilled glass

To a blender, add half of the banana, rice milk, and protein powder. Blend until smooth and pour into the chilled glass.

Rinse the container and then blend the remaining half of the banana, blueberries, orange juice, and blue spirulina.

Pour the vanilla mixture into the tall, chilled glass. Gently pour the blueberry mixture over the top, creating two layers. Garnish with the orange slice and a couple of blueberries. Serve immediately.

The Daphne

Yield: 1 drink
V, V+, GF

Equal parts elegant and intelligent, Daphne Blake is often underestimated by Mystery Inc.'s fearsome foes because of her beauty. She may be a little danger-prone, but when the time comes to solve a case, Daphne always finds a way to sparkle. This lavender Italian soda is just as effervescent as the stylish sleuth that it shares a name with.

LAVENDER-BLACKBERRY SYRUP

1 cup boiling water
1 cup granulated sugar
4 tablespoons culinary lavender buds
2 tablespoons dried butterfly pea flowers
¼ cup fresh blackberries

BLACKBERRY-MINT SODA

2 sprigs mint, divided
1 tablespoon freshly squeezed lemon juice
6 tablespoons Lavender-Blackberry Syrup, divided
Crushed ice
6 to 8 ounces sparkling water
2 blackberries

SPECIAL TOOLS

Muddler
Fine-mesh strainer
Cocktail pick, optional

To make the lavender-blackberry syrup: In a small saucepan, over medium heat, mix the boiling water, sugar, lavender, and pea flowers. Stir until the sugar is completely dissolved and the liquid is clear. Turn off the stove and leave the pot on the heat, steeping for 10 minutes.

Remove the pan from the heat and gently muddle the blackberries in the mixture. Pour through a fine-mesh strainer, reserving the liquid and discarding the solids. Refrigerate and allow to cool completely before using.

The lavender-blackberry syrup can be made ahead and stored in the refrigerator for up to 1 week.

To make the blackberry-mint soda: Using the muddle, combine one sprig of mint with the lemon juice in the bottom of a tall glass. Remove the mint leaves and add 2 tablespoons of the lavender-blackberry syrup. Fill the glass with crushed ice and slowly pour in the sparkling water, leaving about an inch of space at the top.

Thread the blackberries onto the cocktail pick, and spring of mint, if using, to garnish the beverage. Pour the remaining 4 tablespoons of syrup slowly over the back of the spoon, creating a top layer. Serve immediately.

LIQUID SNACKS 95

Jinkies! It's Thai Iced Tea

Yield: 1 drink plus extra coffee jelly
V, GF

When Velma Dinkley is on the case, you know it's going to get solved! Mystery Inc.'s resident genius is laser focused on finding clues. That level of concentration requires a lot of energy, and this iced tea gives her the fuel she needs, thanks to cubes of coffee jelly as thick as her glasses! It's so good it'll have you shouting, "Jinkies!"

COFFEE JELLY
¼ teaspoon coconut oil, for greasing
¾ cup cool coffee
¾ teaspoon agar-agar, see note
6 tablespoons granulated sugar

THAI ICED TEA
¼ diced coffee jelly
Ice
4 ounces Thai tea, made with concentrate or tea bags
2 tablespoons sweetened condensed milk
2 tablespoons heavy whipping cream

SPECIAL TOOLS
Boba straw
Milk frother

To make the coffee jelly: Use the coconut oil and a clean paper towel to grease the bottom of a loaf pan. Set aside.

Pour the coffee in a small saucepan and sprinkle the agar-agar over it. Let it stand for 5 minutes. Place the saucepan over medium-high heat and add the sugar. Cook the mixture, bringing it to a boil, and stir until all the sugar is dissolved and the mixture has thickened, about 3 to 5 minutes. Pour the mixture into the loaf pan and allow to set up for 45 minutes to an hour.

Remove the jelly from the pan, dice into pieces small enough to fit through a boba straw, and store in an airtight container in a cool place or in the refrigerator.

To make the Thai iced tea: Place the coffee jelly in the bottom of a tall glass. Fill the glass with ice and add the Thai tea.

In another tall glass or jar, mix the sweetened condensed milk and cream together with a milk frother until foamy. Carefully pour the cream mixture over the iced tea and serve immediately with a boba straw.

NOTE: Agar-agar is a plant-based substitute for gelatin.

Like, It's Green, Like My Favorite Shirt

Yield: 1 drink
V, GF

When Shaggy Rogers needs to, like, totally chill out after an intense Mystery Inc. mission, he whips up this mellow matcha-white chocolate frozen slushy. Not only is this beverage Shaggy's favorite color, it's topped with some of his favorite snacks. Shaggy suggested using real sardines instead of gummy ones, but we definitely don't recommend that substitution!

6 tablespoons white chocolate chips

½ cup plus 3 tablespoons heavy whipping cream, divided, see tip

1 tablespoon plus ¼ teaspoon matcha powder, divided

1 tablespoon powdered sugar

6 ounces milk of choice

1 cup ice

2 Scooby Snacks, crushed (page 22)

3 Chocolate Covered Sardines (page 15)

SPECIAL TOOLS

Whipped cream canister or hand mixer with a whisk attachment

Blender

In a heat-proof measuring cup or bowl, combine the white chocolate chips with 3 tablespoons of the heavy whipping cream. Cook for 1 minute in the microwave, let stand for 5 minutes, and then stir until smooth. Stir in 1 tablespoon of matcha.

In a whipped cream canister or medium-sized bowl, combine the remaining heavy whipping cream, ¼ teaspoon of matcha, and the powdered sugar.

> **Tip:** If you're not using a whipped cream canister, use a hand mixer with a whisk attachment to whip the cream, on high, until stiff peaks form.

In a blender combine the white chocolate mixture, milk, and ice and blend until smooth.

Immediately pour into a tall glass and top with whipped cream mixture, crushed Scooby Snacks, and Chocolate Covered Sardines.

LIQUID SNACKS

Countess Hagula's Youth Juice

Yield: 1 drink
V, V+, GF

In *Scooby-Doo! Mystery Incorporated*, the Halloween issue of *Celebrity Weekly* featured a drink recipe that could make you look younger than you are. The concoction called for rare ingredients like Star Orchid pollen, cadmium paint, and century-old Bordeaux . . . and it ended up being a big hoax! This healthy alternative won't reverse the effects of time, but it will make you *feel* a lot younger.

1 teaspoon turmeric

2 grinds fresh black pepper, about ⅛ teaspoon

1 cup frozen pineapple chunks, plus 1 piece for garnish

6 ounces coconut milk

1 to 2 teaspoons maple syrup depending on desired sweetness

SPECIAL TOOLS
Blender
Microplane

In a small skillet over medium heat, combine the turmeric and black pepper, and stir for 30 seconds. Remove from the heat and add to a heat-proof container. Stir the spices for another 30 seconds to 1 minute or until fragrant and toasted.

In a blender, combine the toasted spices, 1 cup frozen pineapple, and coconut milk. Blend until smooth. Add the maple syrup to taste and blend briefly to combine.

Pour the smoothie into a tall glass and use a microplane to finely grate the remaining chunk of pineapple over the surface of the smoothie. Serve immediately.

Rock and Roll Ritual Tea

Yield: 1 drink
V, V+, GF

Have you ever screamed so loud that your voice totally gave out? That happens to the members of Mystery Inc. on the regular! Luckily, in *Scooby-Doo! and the Witch's Ghost*, they found the perfect remedy. It's an old Wiccan recipe for peppermint and clove tea that the Hex Girls use before and after every show. The vapors alone are soothing enough, but this warm beverage coats your throat so that you can keep singing—or screaming—all night long!

8 whole cloves

1 mint tea bag

8 ounces boiling water

1 fresh mint sprig

1 to 2 teaspoons honey, depending on desired sweetness level

In a heat-proof mug or glass, add the cloves, tea bag, and boiling water. Steep for 3 to 5 minutes. Remove the tea bag. Add the fresh mint sprig and honey. Stir gently to combine. Allow to cool for 2 or 3 minutes and enjoy.

NOTE: The whole cloves sink to the bottom but caution should still be used while drinking. A small tea infuser can be used to hold the cloves if preferred.

LIQUID SNACKS

Cobweb Potion

Yield: 1 drink
GF

In one of the Hex Girls' biggest hits, the ghoulish goth rockers promise to put a spell on their listeners. Based on their ever-growing legion of adoring fans, it seems to have worked. Was it their signature spooky sound that earned them so much dark devotion? Or was it this little Cobweb Potion that they promised to brew? We may never know . . .

12 ounces milk of choice
4 tablespoons Sweet Double Dutch Chocolate Syrup (page 11)
⅛ teaspoon salt
⅛ teaspoon smoked paprika
¼ teaspoon cinnamon
1 jumbo marshmallow

In a small saucepan or microwavable measuring cup, whisk together the milk, Sweet Double Dutch Chocolate Syrup, salt, paprika, and cinnamon. Heat until just steaming, about 3 to 5 minutes over medium-high heat on the stove or 1 to 2 minutes in the microwave.

Pour into a mug and set aside. In a small, microwave-safe bowl, heat the marshmallow for 10 seconds. Using gloved or slightly greased hands, remove the marshmallow from the bowl and start to pull it apart. Stretch sections of marshmallow across the rim of the mug to create a web-like pattern. Some marshmallows will fall into the hot chocolate; enjoy! Serve immediately.

Plain Iced Tea . . . If It Wasn't for You Muddling Kids!!

Yield: about 4 cups
V, V+, GF

The Mystery Inc. gang usually gets blamed for meddling in the business of the criminals they've caught. Thanks to this recipe, they're about to get accused of *muddling* instead! This refreshing iced tea features peaches and mint perfectly muddled into a mixture that will make even the cruelest criminals stop pointing fingers and start sipping straws.

4 of your favorite iced tea bags, such as a mild black tea, jasmine, or berry

2 cups boiling water

2 tablespoons raw sugar

2 fresh peaches, divided, see note

2 large sprigs mint, plus more for garnish

4 to 6 cups ice

SPECIAL TOOL
Muddler

In a 4-cup, heat-proof container, add the tea bags and the boiling water. Steep for 5 minutes, remove the tea bags, and discard. Add in the sugar and stir until dissolved. Allow to cool for 20 minutes.

While the tea is cooling, peel and slice one of the peaches. Once cool, transfer the tea to a large pitcher, add the sliced peaches and mint sprigs. Use the muddler to macerate and mix the peach and mint together until it is broken up. Fill the pitcher with ice. Serve in tall glasses garnished with additional mint and peach slices, if desired.

Tip: A long wooden spoon can be used in place of a muddler.

This can be made up to a day ahead but muddle the mint and add the ice right before serving.

NOTE: About 1 cup of defrosted frozen peaches can be substituted for the fresh peach for muddling.

LIQUID SNACKS 103

Bubbling Phantom

Yield: 8 servings
V, V+, GF

Mystery Inc. has stopped scores of supernatural spooks over the years, but the most frightening by far is the Phantom Shadow. This grim Green Ghost has come back to haunt the gang on multiple occasions and in multiple forms. However, this Phantom is a cotton candy version that turns this fizzy drink a ghoulish green when it melts!

SYRUP

1 cup water

1 cup granulated sugar

2 ounces ginger, peeled and sliced

1 cinnamon stick

2 star anise

PHANTOMS

1 ¾ ounces caramel apple cotton candy, divided

1 teaspoon bright green edible luster dust, divided

Edible markers, red and black

4 liters sparkling water, well chilled

SPECIAL TOOLS

Fine-mesh strainer

Egg cup with about ¼ cup capacity

To make the syrup: In a medium saucepan, over medium-high heat, combine the water, sugar, ginger, cinnamon, and star anise. Bring the mixture to a boil, stirring to dissolve the sugar. Boil for 2 to 3 minutes, remove from the heat, and let steep for 30 minutes. Pour through a fine-mesh strainer, reserving the syrup and discarding the solids. Refrigerate in an airtight container. This can be made ahead and refrigerated for up to 2 weeks.

To make the phantoms: Gently pull off about ¼ cup of cotton candy. Press the candy into the egg cup, leaving it open in the center. Let the candy extend past the sides of the cup. The edges of your phantom can be rough and torn-looking.

Put ⅛ teaspoon of luster dust into the center of the candy shape and close it up by pressing another small piece of cotton candy over the opening. Gently twist the candy phantom out the egg cup and repeat to create more phantoms. Decorate the phantoms with the edible markers.

The cotton candy will absorb moisture from the environment quickly, so have an airtight container ready to keep your finished phantoms safe. Store the extra cotton candy in its original container, sealed.

In a wide-rimmed glass add 3 tablespoons of the syrup. Top off with about 16 ounces of sparkling water and serve with a candy phantom side. Let guests add the phantom to their own glasses when they're ready to dissolve the mystery of the Bubbling Phantom!

NOTE: This drink can be served over ice but the effect of the swirly phantom dust will be slightly diminished. Instead, chill all ingredients except the phantoms.

CHAPTER 7

Sweet Snacks

Ruh-roh! The party's almost over! But we wouldn't dream of letting you leave without a delightful dessert to end your snacking safari! Mystery Inc. knows how to close a case right, and they've got a wide variety of creepy confections to finish off your frightful feast. These final courses may look scary, but they're really as sweet as can be!

Fruitmeir's Ice Cream

Yield: 6 cones
V*, GF*

As Franklin Fruitmeir says, "It's not ice cream. It's not yogurt. We don't really know what it is!" But we do know that his top-secret recipe was a big hit in *Scooby-Doo! Mystery Incorporated*'s Crystal Cove—even after a local professor used it to disguise himself as a Slime Mutant! This cone of neon goo might look weird, but that doesn't make it any less satisfying!

About 1 tablespoon coconut oil for greasing

6 ounces lime gelatin dessert mix

1 cup very hot water, between 170°F and 200°F

2 cups mini marshmallows

6 scoops vanilla ice cream, about 2 pints

6 ice cream cones, gluten free if desired

SPECIAL TOOLS

3 ½-inch round cookie cutter

Offset spatula

Grease a 9-by-13-inch pan with coconut oil, covering the entire bottom and sides. Set aside.

In a heat-proof measuring cup or bowl, combine the gelatin and the water, stirring until most of the gelatin has dissolved. Add the marshmallows and stir again. Microwave for 30 seconds and then stir until the marshmallow is completely dissolved. If needed, you may microwave again for 10 to 15 seconds, but don't overheat.

Once the mixture is smooth, pour it into the pan and let sit at room temperature, undisturbed, for 1 hour until set.

While the mixture is setting, line a baking tray with parchment and scoop out six scoops of ice cream, placing them on the tray. Keep the scoops small enough to easily fit onto the cones with much overhang. Place the baking tray in the freezer.

Use a 3 ½-inch round cookie cutter to cut circles from the marshmallow mixture and an offset spatula to lift it from the pan. With the greener-side up, drape the marshmallow-lime circles over each scoop of ice cream. Freeze for another 5 minutes and then place each scoop on a cone and serve immediately.

NOTE: This recipe can be gluten free with gluten-free ice cream cones and vegetarian if plant-based gelatin mix is used. Feel free to experiment with different flavors of ice cream or gelatin mix.

Night Sky Tart with Bat Cookies

Yield: about 8 servings

Trouble can rear its ugly head at any time of day, but the members of Mystery Inc. know that night time is the right time for things to go very wrong! Once the moon is out, things tend to get scary, fast. But somehow this tempting tart makes even the darkest night look brighter.

CHOCOLATE CRÉMEUX

- 3 ounces bittersweet chocolate, chopped
- 1 ½ teaspoons vanilla extract
- 1 egg yolk
- 1 tablespoon granulated sugar
- ¼ cup whole milk
- ¼ cup heavy cream

PASTRY

- 1 ¼ cups all-purpose flour
- 6 tablespoons powdered sugar
- ½ teaspoon kosher salt
- ½ cup unsalted butter, very cold
- 2 tablespoons solid vegetable shortening, very cold
- 1 to 2 tablespoons ice water
- 1 tablespoon black cocoa powder
- 1 egg white, mixed with 1 tablespoon water for egg wash
- Edible markers and white and black edible dust, optional

To make the chocolate crémeux: In a heat-proof bowl or 2-cup container, combine the chocolate and vanilla. Set aside.

In a medium bowl, whisk together the egg yolks and sugar until thick and pale, about 3 minutes, then set aside.

In a small, heavy-bottomed saucepan, over medium heat, cook the milk and cream, stirring frequently, until the mixture begins to steam. Remove the pan from the heat, ladle about ⅓ of the milk mixture *slowly* into the eggs, whisking quickly and continuously. This process tempers the eggs, so they don't scramble.

Add the egg mixture back to the saucepan with the remaining milk mixture and return to the stove over medium-low heat. Using the rubber spatula, continue to stir, scraping the bottom and creases of the pan until the mixture thickens. The mixture should be thick enough to fully coat the back of the spatula. This can take up to 30 minutes.

Once the mixture has thickened, remove from the heat and pour over the chocolate. Let it stand for 5 minutes. After 5 minutes, stir the mixture until completely smooth. Cover with plastic wrap touching the surface of the chocolate. Refrigerate for at least 4 hours or preferably overnight. This can be made up to 3 days ahead.

To make the pastries: In the bowl of a food processor, combine the flour, powdered sugar, and salt. Pulse several times. Cut the butter and vegetable shortening into tablespoon-sized chunks and add it to the food processor all at once. Pulse two or three more times, until the mixture resembles a fine sand. Do not overmix. The mixture should be sandy and not stick together at this point.

Drizzle in the ice water 1 tablespoon at a time and pulse three to five times. After each tablespoon, test if the dough is beginning to stick together. Once the dough pieces stick together with your fingers, you've added enough water.

RECIPE CONTINUES ON PAGE 112

SWEET SNACKS

BLACKBERRY SYRUP
10 ounces frozen blackberries
1 cup sugar

BLACKBERRY MOUSSE
3 ounces cream cheese, softened
1 teaspoon balsamic vinegar
5 tablespoons blackberry syrup
½ cup heavy whipping cream

BLACKBERRY GELÉE
4 tablespoons water
1 ½ teaspoons powdered gelatin
7 tablespoons blackberry syrup

SPECIAL TOOLS
Food processor
9-inch tart pan with removable bottom
Pie weights, such as dry beans or rice
Round cookie cutters
Large and small bat cookie cutters
Ghost cookie cutters
Chinois or fine-mesh strainer
Stand mixer fitted with a whisk attachment

Remove about ⅓ of the dough. Wrap it in parchment and set aside. Add the black cocoa powder to remaining dough in the food processor and pulse until it is completely incorporated. Remove the dough from the food processor. Wrap in parchment. Refrigerate all three pieces of dough for at least 1 hour or overnight.

Roll the black dough between two layers of parchment so that it is big enough to overhang the tart pan. Remove one parchment piece. Using the remaining parchment as support, lay the pastry into the tart pan, gently pressing it to the bottom and against the sides. Once the pastry is fitted to the pan, trim off the excess against the edge of the tart pan. If you have any tears, repair by pressing small pieces of dough against them. Refrigerate the tart shell and the rewrapped scraps while you preheat the oven to 400°F.

Line the tart pan with a large piece of foil, making sure it hangs over the edges. Fill the bottom of the pan with pie weights. Bake for 12 minutes, remove from the oven and carefully remove the foil to lift out the weights. With a fork, make numerous pricks on the bottom of the tart shell and brush with the egg wash. Cook for another 10 to 12 minutes or until the pastry is dry and crisp. Allow to cool completely on a wire rack.

While the tart shell is baking, roll out the scraps of the black dough and cut out as many bats as you can in both sizes. Roll out the white dough and cut a large moon and several ghosts. Place all the cutouts on a lined baking sheet and chill for at least 10 minutes. Egg-wash and bake for 8 to 10 minutes until white cookies are a light golden-brown.

Decorate the cookies with the pens and luster dust as desired. Once the cookies have been decorated, they can be stored in an airtight container between layers of parchment for up to 3 days until ready to use.

To make blackberry syrup: In a medium saucepan over low heat, mix the blackberries and sugar, mashing the berries down with a spoon or spatula. Continue stirring until sugar is completely dissolved. Once the sugar has dissolved, turn the heat up to medium and bring to a low boil. Continue to boil, stirring frequently, for about 5 minutes or until mixture has thickened.

> **Tip:** If using fresh blackberries, allow the blackberries to sit in a medium-sized bowl with the sugar and macerate for 30 minutes before adding to the pot.

Remove from the heat and work through the chinois or a fine-mesh strainer to remove all the seeds. Set aside to cool completely.

To make the blackberry mousse: In the bowl of a stand mixer, whip the cream cheese until light and fluffy, approximately 2 minutes. Add the balsamic vinegar and the blackberry syrup. Mix again on high until fully incorporated and fluffy, scraping down the sides of the bowl as needed, approximately 2 to 3 minutes.

In a separate bowl, whip the whipping cream until stiff peaks form. In three batches, gently fold the blackberry mixture into the whipped cream mixture until no streaks remain.

To assemble the tart: Once the tart shell is completely cool, spread the chocolate crémeux over the bottom in an even layer. Top with the blackberry mousse. Make sure to level the mousse out as much as possible and leaving a slight, ⅛-inch gap between the filling and the top of the crust. You may have some extra mousse. Refrigerate for at least 1 hour before adding the gelée.

To make the blackberry gelée: Put 2 tablespoons of water in a small bowl and add gelatin. Set aside and let bloom, about 5 to 10 minutes.

If syrup isn't warm, reheat to approximately 95°F to 105°F. Do not let it boil. Add remaining 2 tablespoons of water and gelatin mixture to warm syrup and stir. Let the gelée mix cool before using.

Pour the gelée across the top of the tart so it covers the mousse in a thin, even layer. Carefully transfer to the refrigerator until it has set, about 30 minutes. At this point you can remove the tart from the pan by gently pushing up from the bottom and letting the ring come away. Place the tart on a cake plate or serving platter and decorate with the pastry cookies. Serve within 30 minutes. Alternatively, you can keep the tart refrigerated for up to 3 days before plating, decorating, and serving.

SWEET SNACKS 113

Spooky Haunted House Cake

Yield: 28 to 32 servings
V

Scooby and the gang spend most of their nights exploring abandoned houses that are rumored to be haunted. Though most of the ghosts turn out to be fakes and frauds, that doesn't make the houses themselves any more welcoming. However, if they were all as delectable as this dessert doppelgänger, it might make midnight missions a lot easier to swallow!

CAKE

3 cups granulated sugar
2 ⅔ cups all-purpose flour
1 ⅓ cups cocoa
1 teaspoon salt
2 ½ teaspoons baking powder
2 ½ teaspoons baking soda
4 eggs
1 cup whole milk
1 tablespoon vanilla extract
1 ½ cups salted butter, melted
1 ¼ cups boiling water

CHOCOLATE–BROWN SUGAR FROSTING

6 egg whites
¼ teaspoon kosher salt
½ cup water
2 cups packed light brown sugar
1 teaspoon lemon juice
3 cups unsalted butter, plus more for greasing
2 teaspoons vanilla extract
4 ounces bittersweet chocolate, melted

To make the cake: Preheat the oven to 350°F. Line three 8-inch round cake pans and two 6-inch round cake pans with rounds of parchment paper. Wrap with cake strips, if using (see note).

Over the bowl of a stand mixer, or a large mixing bowl if using a hand mixer, sift together the sugar, flour, cocoa, salt, baking powder, and baking soda. Using a whisk attachment or hand mixer, mix briefly on low speed.

In a separate medium mixing bowl, whisk together the eggs, milk, vanilla, and melted butter until well-combined. Add the egg mixture to the flour mixture and mix on low speed for 3 minutes. Slowly add in the boiling water and mix on low speed until combined. Make sure to scrape the bottom of the bowl; the batter will be very thin.

Fill each 8-inch pan with 2 cups batter and each 6-inch pan with 1 cup batter. Bake for 15 to 20 minutes or until a cake tester or toothpick comes out clean. Allow the cakes to cool in the pan for 15 minutes. After 15 minutes, run an offset spatula gently around the edge of each cake and turn them out onto wire racks to cool completely.

Either use immediately or wrap each layer in parchment paper and then plastic wrap and refrigerate for 3 days or freeze for 3 weeks. The cake does not have to be defrosted for assembly but should be allowed to come to room temperature for 30 minutes before serving.

To make the chocolate–brown sugar frosting: In the bowl of a stand mixer fitted with a whisk attachment, combine the egg whites and salt; set aside.

> **Tip:** It is not recommended to use a hand mixer with this recipe. The syrup is very hot, and the stability of a stand mixer ensures that you will not spill or splash hot syrup on yourself.

Fit a heavy-bottomed saucepan with a candy thermometer. Over medium-high heat, combine the water and brown sugar and bring to a boil. When the sugar begins to boil, start mixing the egg whites on medium-high speed until frothy. Add the lemon juice to the egg whites and mix, again on medium-high speed, until soft peaks form.

RECIPE CONTINUES ON PAGE 116

SWEET SNACKS

HAUNTED-HOUSE PIECES

½ recipe Coffin Shaker Cookies dough (page 125), see note in the cookie recipe and replace the peppermint with almond or vanilla extract

½ recipe Royal Icing (page 125)

Black and/or green food coloring

½ cup pre-cooked isomalt nibs

1 cup pepitas

½ cup sunflower seeds

Candy rocks, optional

½ cup crushed chocolate wafer cookies, optional "dirt"

½ cup crushed pistachios, optional "moss"

FILLING

1 recipe Sweet Cherry Relish (page 12)

SPECIAL TOOLS

Three 8-inch round cake pans

Two 6-inch round cake pans

Cake strips, optional

Stand mixer or hand mixer fitted with a whisk attachment

Offset spatula

Candy thermometer

Haunted-house template (page 118)

Packing tape

Pastry bag fitted with a large writing tip

NOTE: Just lining the bottom of the pans with parchment and not greasing the whole cake pan allows the batter to climb to its maximum height. Cake strips help prevent domes and result in very level cakes. If you don't use cake strips you will need to trim the domes off your cakes before assembly.

Grease a 2-cup, heat-safe measuring cup with butter.

Continue to boil the sugar until the temperature reaches between 238°F and 242°F on the candy thermometer. Remove from the heat and pour into the greased measuring cup. In small amounts, slowly add the sugar syrup to the egg whites, whisking after each addition. When all the syrup is added, beat the mixture on high speed until the meringue is completely cool. This can take up to 10 minutes. The outside of the bowl should be completely cool to the touch.

Add the butter one piece at a time, beating on medium speed after each addition. Add the vanilla extract and the cooled melted chocolate, beat again on low speed until light and fluffy, 1 to 2 minutes.

To make the haunted-house pieces: Trace the templates onto a piece of paper. Cover the images on both sides with packing tape, and then cut out the templates. The packing tape creates a nonstick surface that can be gently wiped off, making the template easy to reuse.

Roll out the cookie dough to about ⅛ inch thick. Place the templates on the dough and cut out the haunted-house pieces. Cut out two 2 ½-inch squares. Cut one square in half, corner to corner, creating two large triangles. Cut the second square in half the same way and then cut each triangle in half, creating four smaller triangles. These will be your supports for the house pieces. You can reroll the scraps and cut out any extra cookies you may want for decoration such as tombstones, bats, and steps, or you can shape the leftover dough into a spooky tree.

Bake the cookies according to the directions on page 125. Once they are removed from the oven, fill the windows with isomalt, as directed on page 125.

Once the cookies have cooled, use the royal icing to decorate the house pieces and to glue on the pepitas and sunflower seeds for texture and shingles. Decorate any of the other decor cookies you baked. Set the cookies aside to dry for at least 1 hour before carefully storing in an airtight container until needed.

To assemble the cake: Fill a pastry bag fitted with a large writing tip with the chocolate–brown sugar frosting. Place an 8-inch cake layer on a cake board or serving plate and pipe a border of frosting around the edge of the cake. Spread ½ cup Sweet Cherry Relish filling in the center, spreading evenly. Place a second 8-inch layer on top of the first and repeat with another border and more filling. Place the third layer on top and use the frosting to lightly coat the entire cake, filling in the gaps between the layers. This is known as a crumb coat. Refrigerate the cake for 15 minutes.

While the 8-inch cake is in the refrigerator, work with the 6-inch layers. Place one of the layers on a cake board about 1 inch smaller than the cake. Pipe a border of frosting around the edge and fill with about ¼ cup of Sweet Cherry Relish. Place the second layer on top and use the frosting to crumb-coat. Refrigerate for 15 minutes.

Frost both the 8-inch and 6-inch layers completely with frosting and refrigerate for 30 minutes or until ready to decorate. When ready, remove both cakes from the refrigerator. Stack the 6-inch cake on top of the 8-inch cake, setting it off-center and a bit back from the front. Using the brace pieces and more frosting, secure the house pieces on top of the 6-inch cake. Or you can use royal icing to attach the braces and let that dry before placing the house pieces on the cake.

Use the other cookies, candy rocks, and/or more seeds to finish decorating. The cake can sit out at room temperature, around 72°F, for up to 3 hours.

SWEET SNACKS 117

HAUNTED-HOUSE TEMPLATES
Copy at 100%

FRONT LAYER

BACK LAYER

A Trap Cake

Yield: 6 cakes
V

Members of Mystery Inc. are used to finding themselves caught in the middle of nefarious schemes, which means they're also used to finding themselves caught in traps! The gang has been tangled up in giant nets more times than they can count. This net-shaped trap cake serves as a delicious reminder to always keep an eye out for trouble.

TOPPINGS

1 pound strawberries

½ cup dark chocolate melting wafers or chips

Candy eyes, optional

Bone sprinkles, optional

1 tablespoon granulated sugar

2 teaspoons balsamic vinegar

1 cup heavy whipping cream

1 tablespoon powdered sugar

1 teaspoon vanilla extract

4 tablespoons Sweet Double Dutch Chocolate Syrup, divided (page 11)

FUNNEL CAKE DOUGH

1 cup whole milk

½ cup unsalted butter

1 tablespoon granulated sugar

¼ teaspoon salt

2 teaspoons vanilla extract

1 cup all-purpose flour

4 eggs

2 quarts frying oil, such as vegetable, peanut, canola, or safflower

Six 7-by-7-inch squares parchment

About ½ cup powdered sugar, for dusting

SPECIAL TOOLS

Stand mixer fitted with a whisk attachment, hand mixer, or whipped cream canister

Pastry bag fitted with a large pastry tip

To make the toppings: Choose six of the best strawberries. Rinse, pat dry, and hull the stems and line them up on a parchment-lined baking sheet or small cutting board. Melt the chocolate in a microwave-safe container for two 30-second bursts. Let stand for 3 minutes and then stir until smooth. You may need to microwave for another 15 to 30 seconds, but do not overheat.

Using a skewer or fork, dip each strawberry into the chocolate, covering just enough but leaving a space at the top. Let the excess drip off and place on the baking sheet. Decorate with candy eyes and a bone sprinkle for fangs, if using. Set aside to set for about 10 minutes, or refrigerate for faster results.

Slice the remaining strawberries and mix them in a medium bowl with the sugar and balsamic vinegar. Set aside to macerate.

In the bowl of a stand mixer, or large bowl if using a hand mixer, combine the whipping cream, powdered sugar, and vanilla. Whip until stiff peaks form. Refrigerate until needed. Alternatively, fill a whipped cream cannister with the whipped cream, powdered sugar, and vanilla.

To make the funnel cakes: Begin heating the oil in a large Dutch oven or deep fryer. See Fry Station Safety Tips, page 139.

In a large saucepan over medium-high heat, combine the milk, butter, sugar, salt, and vanilla.

Bring to a boil and add the flour all at once. Stir vigorously with a wooden spoon until the mixture is smooth and not sticking to the spoon or the pot. If the mixture looks rough or butter leaks out, just keep stirring until it comes together. When the mixture is smooth and formed into dough, remove it from the heat and transfer it to a bowl.

RECIPE CONTINUES ON PAGE 123

Allow the mixture to cool for 5 minutes and then begin adding the eggs one at a time. Using a wooden spoon, beat after each egg until it is completely incorporated, and the mixture is smooth again. When all the eggs have been added and the mixture is smooth, transfer the mixture to a pastry bag fitted with a large pastry tip.

When the oil temperature is between 360°F and 365°F, begin piping a net-like shape onto each square of parchment. Use only one or two pieces at a time, gently lower the parchment square into the frying oil. As soon as oil coats the surface of the dough, press down on the dough with the rounded side of a spider skimmer, shaping the funnel cake into a basket. The parchment will separate from the cake. Using the skimmer and/or tongs, remove the funnel cakes (and parchment) and transfer to the wire rack, discarding the parchment piece. Dust with powdered sugar and repeat until you have made all six trap cakes.

Place about ¼ cup of the sliced berries on a dessert plate, drizzle with about 2 teaspoons of Sweet Double Dutch Chocolate Syrup, and pipe or dollop whipped cream on top. Place a trap cake over the top and nestle a strawberry monster under the trap. Serve immediately.

NOTE: The trap cakes can be fried and plated to order or keep them warm, without powdered sugar, in a 200°F oven. Dust with powdered sugar just before serving. Leftover components should be stored, separately, in airtight containers in the refrigerator for up to 3 days. Funnel cakes can be stored in an airtight container at room temperature.

SWEET SNACKS

Coffin Shaker Cookies

Yield: about 10 cookies
V

You know what would save the gang a lot of trouble? If they could see what was hiding inside of a creepy coffin without actually having to open it! While most caskets thankfully don't come with windows (for very good reasons), these chocolate coffin cookies clearly show exactly what's within—in this case, candied skulls, bones, and more!

COOKIES
¾ cup salted butter, softened

4 ounces cream cheese, softened

½ cup dark unsweetened cocoa powder

¾ cup granulated sugar

1 egg

½ teaspoon peppermint extract

2 ½ cups all-purpose flour

7 ounces precooked, clear isomalt nibs

Sprinkles, such as bones, eyeballs, bugs, and/or bats

Black edible marker

ROYAL ICING
4 cups powdered sugar, sifted

3 tablespoons meringue powder

6 tablespoons water

Red food coloring

Black food coloring

SPECIAL TOOLS
5-by-3-inch coffin cookie cutter

3-by-2-inch coffin cookie cutter

Stand mixer or hand mixer fitted with the whisk attachment

Three pastry bags fitted with writing tips

To make the cookies: In the bowl of a stand mixer, or a large bowl if using a hand mixer, beat together the butter, cream cheese, cocoa, and sugar until light and fluffy. Add the egg and peppermint and beat again until well-combined. Add the flour 1 cup at a time, mixing on low. With the last cup, mix by hand. Split the dough in half, form into disks, wrap in parchment paper, and chill for at least 1 hour. Toward the end of the hour, preheat the oven to 375°F.

After chilling the dough, work with one half at a time on a lightly floured silicone mat. Roll out each disk to ⅛ inch thick. Cut out as many of the large coffins as possible. For every three coffins, use the small cookie cutter to cut a window out of two. You can either reroll the small coffins or bake them to be decorated in an alternate way.

Slide a baking sheet under the silicone mat, rewrap the scraps, and chill both the scraps and the cookies while working with the second disk. Repeat with the second disk and make sure the cookies chill for at least 10 minutes before baking.

Bake the cookies for 9 to 12 minutes or until they feel firm on the surface. Remove from the oven and allow to cool for a few minutes before transferring to a cool baking sheet covered in parchment. Melt the isomalt nibs in a heat-proof measuring cup in the microwave for 1 minute. Check to see if the isomalt is completely melted and bubbling, if not, continue to cook in 30-second bursts.

For every set of three coffins, fill the center window of one with isomalt. Bang the baking sheet several times on a firm surface and/or use a toothpick to pop and remove bubbles. The isomalt cools quickly so you may need to reheat, 30 seconds at a time, periodically. Repeat until all the sets have one candy window cookie, one empty spacer cookie, and one base coffin cookie. Set aside until the isomalt is set, about 10 minutes. If not decorating immediately, store in an airtight container between layers of parchment.

RECIPE CONTINUES ON PAGE 126

NOTE: This dough is very flexible and pairs well with many flavorings; replace the peppermint with ½ teaspoon of almond extract, ¼ teaspoon of lemon or orange, or a teaspoon of vanilla. The cookies can be baked ahead and frozen for up to 1 month before decorating. There is no need to defrost before decorating.

To make the royal icing: In the bowl of a stand mixer fitted with the whisk attachment, combine the powdered sugar, meringue powder, and water. Whisk on low speed for 7 to 10 minutes, or until the icing holds stiff peaks. (If using a hand mixer, whisk on high speed for 10 to 12 minutes.)

Divide the icing into two or three small bowls and dye one red, one black, and leave one white, if desired. Transfer some of each color to a pastry bag fitted with writing tips. Transfer the remaining icing to airtight containers or cover the bowls with plastic wrap.

To assemble, line the blank large coffin cookies with the red or white icing across the surface of the cookies. Using a clean craft brush dipped in water, create a thin layer of the frosting. Let this dry for at least 30 minutes.

Decorate the inside of the coffin by using the black edible marker to create designs such as scratch marks or more. You can also decorate the inside of the coffin windows by drawing vines, bats, or branches.

Use the black royal icing to glue each spacer cookie onto a coffin base cookie by piping a thin line of icing around the edge. Allow to dry for at least 1 hour.

Once the cookies have dried, spoon about ½ teaspoon of sprinkles into the center of the spacer cookie. Using the same black royal icing, glue the candy window cookies onto the spacers. Do not disturb for another hour or your sprinkles will get caught in the icing. Use additional icing to decorate the outside of the coffins. Allow to dry for another 30 to 60 minutes depending on the amount of icing.

Once completely dry, store in an airtight container between layers of parchment or individually wrap in cellophane bags for gifting. Cookies can be stored for about 5 days.

Jellied Eyeball Cobbler

Yield: 6 to 8 servings
V, GF*

The Bloody Stake's "All You Can Gorge Night" is a challenge that pro diners like Shaggy and Scooby can't resist in *Scooby-Doo! Mystery Incorporated*. We don't recommend using the duos "All Gulp, No Air" eating technique—after all, if you did that, you wouldn't have any room left for one of the Stake's signature desserts. This bizarre blueberry cobbler is the perfect way to finish off any meal, no matter how massive!

FILLING

1 ¼ pounds blueberries, picked over and rinsed
One 20-ounce can whole lychees
2 tablespoons fresh lime juice
2 ½ tablespoons tapioca flour
½ cup granulated sugar
2 tablespoons Sweet Cherry Relish (page 11)

TOPPING

1 cup all-purpose flour
¾ cup oats
¾ cup granulated sugar
½ cup light brown sugar
½ teaspoon salt
½ teaspoon ground ginger
1 tablespoon black cocoa powder
¾ cup unsalted butter

SPECIAL TOOLS

Muffin tin or deviled egg plate
9- or 10-inch pie plate, at least 2 inches deep

NOTE: *This recipe works well with your favorite cup for cup gluten-free flour and gluten-free oats.

Preheat the oven to 375°F.

To make the filling: Drain the lychee, reserving ¼ cup of juice and all the fruit. Sort through the lychees and choose the best eight to ten, set aside. Mince the remaining leeches.

In a large bowl combine the reserved lychee juice, lime juice, tapioca flour, sugar, blueberries, and minced lychee. Stir to thoroughly combine.

In the cavities of a mini muffin tin or deviled egg plate, place the whole lychees. Fill each one with a small amount of relish, about ¼ teaspoon. Pulling from the filling, place a blueberry into each lychee, pressing down gently. Set the prepared eyes aside.

To make the topping: In a medium bowl, combine the flour, oats, sugars, salt, ginger, and black cocoa. Cut the butter into tablespoon-sized pieces. Use a pastry cutter or two butter knives to mix in the butter, until the pieces are pea-sized.

In the pie pan, pour the filling and level with a spoon. Sprinkle the topping over the fruit. Press down slightly to completely cover the filling, all the way to the edges of the pie pan.

Bake for 25 minutes, remove from the oven, and add the lychee eyeballs, pressing them into the topping. Return to the oven and bake for another 20 to 25 minutes or until the fruit is bubbling.

Tip: During the second bake, you may want to place a foil-lined baking sheet under the pie pan to catch any drips.

Allow to cool for 10 to 15 minutes if serving warm. The cobbler can also be cooled completely, covered, and refrigerated for up to 3 days. Serve plain, with loose or whipped cream, or ice cream.

SWEET SNACKS

Scooby-Doo Cookie Tags

Yield: about 32 cookies
V

Scooby-Doo's yellow-and-blue dog tag is nearly as iconic as Scooby himself. This diamond-shaped charm emblazoned with his initials is the only accessory this crime-solving canine needs to look cool! These edible replicas are just as fashionable as the real thing—and a thousand times yummier!

DOUGH
¾ cup salted butter, softened
4 ounces cream cheese, softened
¾ cup granulated sugar
1 egg
1 teaspoon vanilla extract
3 cups all-purpose flour
Royal blue food coloring

TOPPINGS
½ recipe Royal Icing (page 125)
Yellow food coloring
Blue licorice or sour belts, optional

SPECIAL TOOLS
Hand mixer or stand mixer fitted with a paddle attachment
2-inch square cookie cutter
Pastry bag fitted with a writing tip

To make the dough: Using a stand mixer fitted with a paddle attachment, or a large bowl if using a hand mixer, beat together the butter, cream cheese, and sugar until light and fluffy. Add the egg and vanilla and beat again until well-combined. Add the flour 1 cup at a time, mixing on low. At the last cup of flour, mix the dough by hand. Add the food coloring to the dough and knead it in by hand, until it is evenly dyed the color of Scooby's tag. Wearing gloves is the best way to do this, but if you don't have gloves, kneading while it is in a resealable bag will work.

Split the dough in half, form into disks, wrap in parchment paper, and chill for at least 1 hour. Toward the end of the hour, preheat the oven to 375°F.

Once the dough is chilled, lightly flour a silicone mat. Working with one disk at a time, roll out each disk to ⅛ inch thick. Cut as many squares as you can. If you are planning on using the licorice laces, use the end of a chop stick to poke a hole in one corner of each cookie. This will become the top of the diamond shape of Scooby's tag. Slide a baking sheet under the silicone mat and rewrap the scraps. Chill both the scraps and the cookies while working with the second disk.

Repeat with the second disk and make sure the cookies chill for at least 10 minutes before baking. Bake for 10 to 12 minutes or until just starting to brown at the edges. Allow to cool on a wire rack.

To decorate: Dye the royal icing yellow, load it into the pastry bag, and decorate the cookies to create a border and Scooby's initials. Allow to dry for about 1 hour. Store between layers of parchment in an airtight container or package in the cellophane bags. If using, thread a 5-inch length of licorice lace through the tag.

Bat Macarons

Yield: about 12 macarons
V, GF

What's that swooping through the sky? You'd better bet it's a bat! Whether the gang is lost in the woods or exploring an attic, bats are bound to swoop out and surround them at any moment. Instead of fleeing in fear, it's time to celebrate the things that go flap in the night with these magnificent macarons!

MACARONS
½ cup fine, blanched almond flour
1 ½ tablespoons dark cocoa powder
1 ½ tablespoons black cocoa powder
1 cup powdered sugar
2 egg whites
⅛ teaspoon cream of tartar
¼ cup superfine sugar
½ teaspoon vanilla extract

GANACHE
¼ cup semi-sweet chocolate chips
3 tablespoons heavy whipping cream
½ tablespoon unsalted butter
¼ teaspoon almond extract

FILLING
¼ cup raspberry jam

SPECIAL TOOLS
Food processor
Stand mixer or hand mixer fitted with a whisk attachment
Two pastry bags fitted with medium writing tips
Bat template (page 131)

To make the macarons: In the bowl of a food processor, mix the almond flour, cocoa powders, and powdered sugar and run for about 1 minute. You may need to pulse to combine. Sift over a large bowl, twice. After two siftings, you may discard up to 1 teaspoon of solids.

In the bowl of a stand mixer fitted with a whisk attachment, or a large mixing bowl if using a hand mixer, combine the egg whites and the cream of tartar. Whisk on high speed until soft peaks form. With the mixer running, slowly sprinkle in the superfine sugar and continue to whisk until stiff peaks form. The meringue should hold a point when the whisk is pulled away from it.

To the almond mixture, add vanilla and the meringue all at once. Use a rubber spatula to slowly pull the meringue through the almond mixture. (This process is called macaronage.) The mixture should be fully combined but keep a bit of stiffness. Do not overmix and let the batter get to what is called the ribbon stage, where everything is thoroughly blended.

Preheat the oven to 375°F and line two baking sheets with parchment paper. Fit the pastry bag with the tip and fill with the macaron mixture.

Slide the template under the parchment, trace the outline of the bat with the batter and then fill. Allowing about an inch between, slide the template to the next position, and repeat until you have filled the tray.

Tap the tray once or twice to help remove air bubbles and let rest for 15 minutes. While the first tray is resting, begin piping the second tray. Reduce the oven to 325°F and bake for 10 to 13 minutes or until dry and crisp. Once the first batch has been removed from the oven, allow the second tray to rest for 15 minutes, and reheat the oven to 375°F. Reduce the oven back to 325°F right before you put the second tray in the oven.

Allow all the shells to cool completely before storing in an airtight container while you make the ganache.

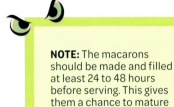

NOTE: The macarons should be made and filled at least 24 to 48 hours before serving. This gives them a chance to mature and have a chewy interior with a crisp exterior that they are known for.

To make the ganache: In a microwave-safe bowl, add the chocolate and cover with the whipping cream. Microwave for 1 minute and leave standing in the microwave for 5 more minutes. Remove from the microwave, add the butter, and stir until smooth. Add the almond extract and stir to incorporate. Refrigerate for 45 to 60 minutes until firm but still spreadable.

To fill, pair up the macarons and use the edible pens and luster dust to decorate the top bat of each set. Place the ganache into a piping bag fitted with a medium writing tip and pipe a circle of ganache around the edge of each bottom macaron. Fill the centers of the circle with jam and top with another macaron. Store refrigerated in an airtight container between layers of parchment for up to 3 days.

BAT MACARON TEMPLATE
Copy at 100%

SWEET SNACKS

Headless Horseman Pastries

Yield: about 12 pastries
V

The Headless Horseman may seem like nothing more than an old folktale. But for a hot second, Mystery Inc. thought this fabled fiend had leapt straight out of the storybooks to wreak havoc in the real world in *The Scooby-Doo Show* and on other creepy cases. The Horseman they encountered turned out not to be the real deal, but this pumpkin puff pastry is the stuff of legends!

One 17-ounce box puff pastry, defrosted according to package directions
8 ounces mascarpone cheese
1 cup pumpkin puree
¼ cup dark brown sugar
1 teaspoon cinnamon
¼ teaspoon nutmeg
¼ teaspoon clove
1 teaspoon ginger
¾ cup granulated sugar
Black edible marker
¼ cup water
Orange food coloring
2 to 3 drops cinnamon oil or ¼ teaspoon cinnamon extract

SPECIAL TOOLS
One 3 ½-inch pumpkin cookie cutter
Instant candy or fry thermometer
Pastry bag fitted with a long pastry tip

NOTE: For a more make-ahead version, prepare the pastries, cover with their sugar layer, and store at room temperature in an airtight container between layers of parchment. Create the filling and store it in the refrigerator. Assemble right before or up to a few hours before serving. The pastry has no egg wash because it interferes with the sugar coating.

Lay the puff pastry out on the lightly floured surface. Use the pumpkin cookie cutter to cut out shapes as possible. Prepare two baking sheets with a silicone mat or parchment paper and place the pumpkins on both. Note that scraps can be re-rolled but they will not puff quite as much as the original sheets of puff pastry.

Refrigerate the cut-out pumpkins while you preheat the oven to 400°F. Bake the pastry for 10 to 12 minutes or until golden-brown and well-puffed. Remove from the oven and allow to cool completely on a wire rack.

While the pastry is cooling, combine the mascarpone cheese, pumpkin puree, brown sugar, cinnamon, nutmeg, clove, and ginger in a medium bowl. Beat together with a rubber spatula until well-combined. Cover and refrigerate until needed.

Once the pastry is cool, draw the headless horseman's face onto each pastry with the edible marker. Set aside.

In a 2-cup capacity, heavy-bottomed saucepan, pour the granulated sugar into the center. Pour water around the edge of the sugar and place over medium heat. Using a high-heat spatula or wooden spoon, gently draw the water across the surface of the sugar until it is moistened. Do not stir! Add the orange food coloring and cinnamon flavoring. Continue to pull the spoon through the sugar until most of it has dissolved. Cover the pan with a tight-fitting lid and cook undisturbed for 2 minutes. Remove the lid, if the mixture is not boiling, and turn the heat up a bit. Using an instant candy or fry thermometer, boil the sugar mixture until it reaches 300°F. Immediately remove from the heat.

Holding the pumpkin pastries carefully from the bottom, dip the very top into the sugar, covering it with a thin coating. Allow the excess to drip off before returning the pastry to the baking sheet. Alternatively, you can use tongs to hold the back of the pastries. If the sugar mixture becomes too thick to create an even, thin coat, place the pan back on the stove, over medium heat, swirling constantly for about 30 seconds. Continue until you have coated all the pastries. Allow the sugar to set for 5 to 10 minutes.

Put the filling in a pastry bag fitted with a long pastry tip. Poke the pastry tip into the side of a pastry and fill it with the pumpkin mixture. Stop when the pastry becomes heavy and a bit of the filling comes out of the opening. Be careful not to overfill or fill too fast and burst the sides of the pastry. Serve immediately.

Leftovers can be stored in an airtight container in the refrigerator between layers of parchment for up to 1 day.

It's a Clue! Panna Cotta

Yield: 6 panna cottas
GF

When the gang finds themselves hot on the heels of creeps and crooks, Velma quickly whips out her trusty magnifying glass to search for evidence. This panna cotta pays homage to her trusty tool, highlighting a nutty footprint path beneath a layer of transparent gelée. If you can't see how good this one is, you haven't got a clue!

PANNA COTTA
- 2 ½ cups half-and-half, divided
- 2 teaspoons powdered gelatin
- ¼ cup granulated sugar
- Pinch kosher salt
- 6 ounces semisweet chocolate pieces
- 3 ounces dark chocolate pieces
- 1 teaspoon vanilla extract
- ½ teaspoon instant espresso
- 24 to 30 very green roasted whole pistachios, shelled

PHANTOM SYRUP GELÉE
- 1 ½ cups Bubbling Phantom syrup (page 104)
- 4 teaspoons powdered gelatin

SPECIAL TOOLS
Six 8-ounce serving dishes or bowls

To make the panna cotta: Place ¼ cup of half-and-half in a small bowl and sprinkle the gelatin across the surface. Set aside and let bloom.

In a heavy-bottomed medium saucepan over medium heat, combine the remaining 2 ¼ cups half-and-half, the sugar, and a pinch of salt. Stir until the sugar dissolves and bubbles form around the edges, about 7 to 10 minutes.

Add the chocolate and espresso powder and stir until chocolate is melted and the mixture is smooth and uniform in color. Remove from heat and mix in the vanilla and gelatin mixture. Stir until the gelatin is completely dissolved.

Place the serving dishes on a small-rimmed cookie sheet. Pour about 6 ounces of the chocolate mixture in each of the dishes, leaving at least ½ inch of room at the top. Cover each ramekin with plastic wrap, making sure not to touch the surfaces. Place the sheet in the refrigerator for the panna cotta to set up for a minimum of 30 minutes.

While panna cotta sets, prepare the decorations. Slice off approximately ¼ of one end of each pistachio to create the heel of the footprint. The longer piece will be the toe of the foot and the shorter piece, when turned onto its cut side, will become the heel.

To decorate, place the two nut pieces in an alternating pattern to the left then right of an imaginary line down the center of the set panna cotta. Gently press the nut footprints onto the surface of the panna cotta.

To make the phantom syrup gelée: In a medium bowl, pour ¼ cup of the simple syrup and sprinkle the powdered gelatin across the surface. Set aside and let bloom for 5 to 10 minutes.

In a small saucepan, over medium-low heat, warm the remaining syrup to approximately 95°F to 105°F but do not boil. Stir the gelatin mixture into the warmed syrup mixture. Continue to stir until the gelatin is cool enough to not melt the surface of the chocolate layer of the panna cotta, about 10 minutes. Gently spoon approximately 3 to 4 tablespoons on each dessert to cover the pistachio footprints. Make sure the pistachio nuts are not floating before the gelée layer sets. Return the desserts to the refrigerator and allow them to set for at least 15 minutes.

SWEET SNACKS 135

Suggested Menus

Scooby-Doo Watch Party

- Scooby Snacks
- Scooby Snack Mix
- Secret Silo Popcorn
- Mini Burgers in a Pile
- Chocolate Covered Sardines
- Scooby Shake (and Shiver)
- Zoinks! It's a Shaggy Shake
- Scooby-Doo Cookie Tags

Haunted Halloween Boogie

- Spooky Layer Dip
- Chili Snacks
- Fried Moonbeams
- Eyeball Bites
- Rizza Rie with Cherry Sauce
- Spooky Haunted House Cake or Bat Macarons and Headless Horseman Pastries
- Bubbling Phantom

Hex Girls Listening Party

- Super Garlic Food
- Goth Bites
- Sinister Spaghetti or Hex Fire Chili
- Cobweb Potion
- Rock and Roll Ritual Tea
- Coffin Shaker Cookies
- Night Sky Tart with Bat Cookies

Mystery-Solving Dinner Party

- Caprese Skull Salad
- Crawling Potato Beetles
- Mummy Wrappings
- Creepy Crab Brûlée
- Stakeout? I'd Rather Have a Steak In!
- The Daphne
- Plain Iced Tea . . . If It Wasn't for You Muddling Kids!!
- A Trap Cake or It's a Clue! Panna Cotta

Groovy Gathering

- Spicy Funky Fritters
- Finger (and Toe) Fries
- Hot Dog Tacos with All the Trimmings
- Super-Duper Hero Sandwich
- Like, It's Green, Like My Favorite Shirt
- Fruitmeir's Ice Cream
- Jellied Eyeball Cobbler

Mystery Machine Stakeout Snacks

- Scooby Snack Mix
- Mellow Mutt Munchies
- Werewolf Snacks, Chunky-Style
- Ham Sandwich (to Calm My Nerves)
- Looks Like We Got Ourselves a Protein Shake
- Jinkies! It's Thai Iced Tea

Measurement Conversions

Kitchen Measurements

CUP	TABLESPOON	TEASPOON	FLUID OUNCES
1/16 cup	1 tablespoon	3 teaspoons	½ fluid ounce
⅛ cup	2 tablespoons	6 teaspoons	1 fluid ounce
¼ cup	4 tablespoons	12 teaspoons	2 fluid ounces
⅓ cup	5⅓ tablespoons	16 teaspoons	2⅔ fluid ounces
½ cup	8 tablespoons	24 teaspoons	4 fluid ounces
⅔ cup	10⅔ tablespoons	32 teaspoons	5⅓ fluid ounces
¾ cup	12 tablespoons	36 teaspoons	6 fluid ounces
1 cup	16 tablespoons	48 teaspoons	8 fluid ounces

GALLON	QUART	PINT	CUP	FLUID OUNCES
1/16 gallon	¼ quart	½ pint	1 cup	8 fluid ounces
⅛ gallon	½ quart	1 pint	2 cups	16 fluid ounces
¼ gallon	1 quart	2 pints	4 cups	32 fluid ounces
½ gallon	2 quarts	4 pints	8 cups	64 fluid ounces
1 gallon	4 quarts	8 pints	16 cups	128 fluid ounces

Oven Temperatures

CELCIUS	FAHRENHEIT
93°C	200°F
107°C	225°F
121°C	250°F
135°C	275°F
149°C	300°F
163°C	325°F
177°C	350°F
191°C	375°F
204°C	400°F
218°C	425°F
232°C	450°F

Weight

GRAMS	OUNCES
14 grams	½ ounce
28 grams	1 ounce
57 grams	2 ounces
85 grams	3 ounces
113 grams	4 ounces
142 grams	5 ounces
170 grams	6 ounces
283 grams	10 ounces
397 grams	14 ounces
454 grams	16 ounces
907 grams	32 ounces

Length

METRIC	IMPERIAL
2½ centimeters	1 inch
5 centimeters	2 inches
10 centimeters	4 inches
15 centimeters	6 inches
20 centimeters	8 inches
25 centimeters	10 inches
30 centimeters	12 inches

Dietary Considerations

Double Dutch Chocolate Syrup .... V, V+, GF

Sweet Cherry Relish .... V, V+, GF

Bayou Pierre's Hot Sauce................ V, V+, GF

Chocolate Covered Sardines .... V, GF*

Toadstool Toppers .... V, GF

Mozzarella Skulls .... V, GF

Scooby Snacks........................... V

Scooby Snack Mix V

Mellow Mutt Munchies .... V*, GF*

Secret Silo Popcorn .... V, GF

Chili Snacks .... V, V+*, GF*

Pickled Vampire Wings .... V, V+, GF

Werewolf Snacks, Chunky-Style .... GF

Fried Moonbeams .... V, GF

Spooky Layer Dip .... V, GF

Crawling Potato Beetles .... V, GF

Caprese Skull Salad .... V, GF

Super Garlic Food .... GF

Spicy Funky Fritters .... V, GF

Finger (and Toe) Fries................... V, V+, GF

Eyeball Bites V

Mummy Wrappings..................... V*

Zucchini Zombies V

Creepy Crab Brûlée

C.R.U.S.T. Sticky Situation V

Save Breakfast! .... GF

Ghost Pirate Stew .... GF

Sinister Spaghetti V

Rizza Rie with Cherry Sauce

Stakeout? I'd Rather Have a Steak In! .... GF

Hex Fire Chili .... V, V+*, GF

Hot Dog Tacos with All the Trimmings ... GF*

Jeepers! It's the Creeper Dog .... V*, GF

Mini Burgers in a Pile

Goth Bites V

Super-Duper Hero Sandwich

Triple-Decker Veggie Club .... V, V+*, GF*

Ham Sandwich (to Calm My Nerves)

Jaw-Stretcher Special

Hot Pepper Po' Boy

Scooby Shake (and Shiver) .... V, GF*

Zoinks! It's a Shaggy Shake .... GF

Looks Like We Got Ourselves
a Protein Shake .... V, V+, GF

The Daphne .... V, V+, GF

Jinkies! It's Thai Iced Tea .... V, GF

Like, It's Green, Like My Favorite Shirt.... V, GF

Countess Hagula's Youth Juice .... V, V+, GF

Rock and Roll Ritual Tea .... V, V+, GF

Cobweb Potion .... GF

Plain Iced Tea ... If It Wasn't for
You Muddling Kids!! .... V, V+, GF

Bubbling Phantom . . . . V, V+, GF

Fruitmeir's Ice Cream . . . . V*, GF*

Night Sky Tart with Bat Cookies

Spooky Haunted House Cake V

A Trap Cake V

Coffin Shaker Cookies V

Jellied Eyeball Cobbler . . . . V, GF*

Scooby-Doo Cookie Tags V

Bat Macarons . . . . V, GF

Headless Horseman Pastries V

It's a Clue! Panna Cotta . . . . GF

Key:

V = Vegetarian

V* = Easily Made Vegetarian

V+ = Vegan

V+* = Easily Made Vegan

GF = Gluten free

GF*= Easily Made Gluten free

Fry Station Safety Tips

If you're making something that requires deep-frying, here are some important tips to prevent any kitchen fires:

- If you don't have a dedicated deep fryer, use a Dutch oven or a high-walled sauté pan.

- Never have too much oil in the pan! You don't want hot oil spilling out as soon as you put the food in.

- Only use a suitable cooking oil, like safflower, peanut, or vegetable oil.

- Always keep track of the oil temperature with a thermometer—350°F to 375°F should do the trick.

- Never put too much food in the pan at the same time!

- Never put wet food in the pan. It will splatter and may cause burns.

- Always have a lid nearby to cover the pan in case it starts to spill over or catch fire. A properly rated fire extinguisher is also great to have on hand in case of emergencies.

- Never leave the pan unattended and never let children near the pan.

- Never, ever touch the hot oil.

Index

A

Almond flour/meal
    Bat Macarons, 130–31
    Double Dutch Chocolate Syrup, 11
Anchovies
    Rizza Rie with Cherry Sauce, 60
Apricots
    Werewolf Snacks, Chunky-Style, 31
Avocados
    Corn Salsa, 65
    Crema, 63
    Triple-Decker Veggie Club, 79

B

Bacon
    Save Breakfast!, 56
    Zoinks! It's a Shaggy Shake, 91
Bananas
    Eyeball Bites, 45
    Looks Like We Got Ourselves a Protein Shake, 92
Basil
    Caprese Skull Salad, 40
    Dusk's pesto sandwiches, 74
Bat Cookies, Night Sky Tart with, 111–13
Bat Macarons, 130–31
Bayou Pierre's Hot Sauce, 13
Beans
    Hex Fire Chili, 63
    Spooky Layer Dip, 35
Beef
    Jaw-Stretcher Special, 82
    Mini Burgers in a Pile, 69
    Stakeout? I'd Rather Have Steak In!, 62
Beetles, Crawling Potato, 38
Beets
    Sinister Spaghetti, 59
Blackberries
    The Daphne, 95
    Luna's blackberry-carrot sandwich, 73
Blueberries
    Jellied Eyeball Cobbler, 127
    Looks Like We Got Ourselves a Protein Shake, 92
Bubbling Phantom, 104
Burgers, Mini, in a Pile, 69

C

Cakes
    Spooky Haunted House Cake, 115–19
    A Trap Cake, 120–23
Caprese Skull Salad, 40
Carrots
    Crawling Potato Beetles, 38
    Luna's blackberry-carrot sandwich, 73
    Sinister Spaghetti, 59
Cheese
    Caprese Skull Salad, 40
    Creepy Crab Brûlée, 50
    Dusk's pesto sandwiches, 74
    Fried Moonbeams, 32
    Ham Sandwich (to Calm My Nerves), 81
    Headless Horseman Pastries, 132
    Hot Dog Tacos with All the Trimmings, 65
    Jaw-Stretcher Special, 82
    Luna's blackberry-carrot sandwich, 73
    Mini Burgers in a Pile, 69
    Mozzarella Skulls, 19
    Mummy Wrappings, 46–47
    Rizza Rie with Cherry Sauce, 60
    Save Breakfast!, 56
    Sinister Spaghetti, 59
    Spooky Layer Dip, 35
    Super-Duper Hero Sandwich, 75
    Triple-Decker Veggie Club, 79
    Zucchini Zombies, 49
Cherries
    Night Sky Tart, with Bat Cookies, 111–13
    Rizza Rie with Cherry Sauce, 60
    Scooby Snack Mix, 25
    Spooky Haunted House Cake, 115–19
    Sweet Cherry Relish, 12
Chicken
    Werewolf Snacks, Chunky-Style, 31
Chili, Hex Fire, 63
Chili peppers
    Bayou Pierre's Hot Sauce, 13
    Double Dutch Chocolate Syrup, 11
    Hex Fire Chili, 63
    Hot Pepper Po' Boy, 85
    Spicy Funky Fritters, 42
Chili Snacks, 29
Chocolate. *See also* White chocolate
    Bat Macarons, 130–31
    Chocolate Covered Sardines, 15
    Cobweb Potion, 102
    Coffin Shaker Cookies, 125–26
    Double Dutch Chocolate Syrup, 11
    It's a Clue! Panna Cotta, 135
    Night Sky Tart, with Bat Cookies, 111–13
    Scooby Shake (and Shiver), 88
    Scooby Snack Mix, 25
    Scooby Snacks, 22
    Spooky Haunted House Cake, 115–19
    Thorn's raspberry-rose sandwich, 72
    A Trap Cake, 120–23
    Zoinks! It's a Shaggy Shake, 91
Cilantro
    Crema, 63
    Hot Dog Tacos with All the Trimmings, 65
Cinnamon
    Bubbling Phantom, 104
    Mellow Mutt Munchies, 26
    Scooby Snacks, 22
Cloves
    Rock and Roll Ritual Tea, 101
Cobbler, Jellied Eyeball, 127
Cobweb Potion, 102
Coffee
    Jinkies! It's Thai Iced Tea, 96
Coffin Shaker Cookies, 125–26
Cookies
    Coffin Shaker Cookies, 125–26
    Night Sky Tart, with Bat Cookies, 111–13
    Scooby Doo Cookie Tags, 128
    Scooby Snacks, 22
Corn Salsa, 65
Cotton candy
    Bubbling Phantom, 104
Countess Hagula's Youth Juice, 100
Crab Brûlée, Creepy, 50
Crawling Potato Beetles, 38
Creepy Crab Brûlée, 50
Crema, 63
C.R.U.S.T. Sticky Situation, 54
Currants
    Eyeball Bites, 45

D

The Daphne, 95
Deep-frying safety tips, 139
Dips
    Corn Salsa, 65
    Spooky Layer Dip, 35
Double Dutch Chocolate Syrup, 11
Drinks
    Bubbling Phantom, 104
    Cobweb Potion, 102
    Countess Hagula's Youth Juice, 100
    The Daphne, 95
    Jinkies! It's Thai Iced Tea, 96
    Like, It's Green, Like My Favorite Shirt, 99
    Looks Like We Got Ourselves a Protein Shake, 92
    Plain Iced Tea . . . If It Wasn't for You Muddling Kids!!, 103
    Rock and Roll Ritual Tea, 101
    Scooby Shake (and Shiver), 88
    Zoinks! It's a Shaggy Shake, 91
Dusk's pesto sandwiches, 74

E

Eggplant
    Super Garlic Food, 41
Eggs
    Save Breakfast!, 56
Eyeball Bites, 45
Eyeball Cobbler, Jellied, 127

F

Finger (and Toe) Fries, 43
French toast
    C.R.U.S.T. Sticky Situation, 54
Fried Moonbeams, 32
Fries, Finger (and Toe), 43
Fritters, Spicy Funky, 42
Fruitmeir's Ice Cream, 108
Fry station safety tips, 139

G

Garlic
    Pickled Vampire Wings, 30
    Super Garlic Food, 41
Ghost Pirate Stew, 57
Ginger
    Bubbling Phantom, 104
Goth Bites, 72–74
Grapes
    Mummy Wrappings, 46–47
Groovy Gathering menu, 136
Guacamole
    Spooky Layer Dip, 35
Gummy fish
    Chocolate Covered Sardines, 15

H

Ham Sandwich (to Calm My Nerves), 81
Haunted Halloween Boogie menu, 136
Haunted House Cake, Spooky, 115–19
Headless Horseman Pastries, 132
Hero Sandwich, Super-Duper, 75
Hex Fire Chili, 63
Hex Girls Listening Party menu, 136
Hot dogs
    Hot Dog Tacos with All the Trimmings, 65
    Jeepers! It's the Creeper Dog, 66
Hot Pepper Po' Boy, 85
Hot Sauce, Bayou Pierre's, 13

I

Ice cream
    Fruitmeir's Ice Cream, 108
    Scooby Shake (and Shiver), 88
    Zoinks! It's a Shaggy Shake, 91
It's a Clue! Panna Cotta, 135

J

Jam
    Bat Macarons, 130–31
    C.R.U.S.T. Sticky Situation, 54
Jaw-Stretcher Special, 82
Jeepers! It's the Creeper Dog, 66
Jellied Eyeball Cobbler, 127
Jinkies! It's Thai Iced Tea, 96

K

Kale
    Pickled Vampire Wings, 30

L

Lavender
    The Daphne, 95
Like, It's Green, Like My Favorite Shirt, 99
Looks Like We Got Ourselves a Protein Shake, 92
Luna's blackberry-carrot sandwich, 73
Lychees
    Jellied Eyeball Cobbler, 127

M

Macarons, Bat, 130–31
Marshmallows
    Cobweb Potion, 102
    Fruitmeir's Ice Cream, 108
    Mellow Mutt Munchies, 26
    Scooby Snacks, 22
Matcha powder
    Like, It's Green, Like My Favorite Shirt, 99
Mellow Mutt Munchies, 26
Menus, suggested, 136
Meringues
    Bat Macarons, 130–31
    Toadstool Toppers, 16–17
Mini Burgers in a Pile, 69
Mint
    The Daphne, 95
    Plain Iced Tea . . . If It Wasn't for You Muddling Kids!!, 103
    Rock and Roll Ritual Tea, 101
Moonbeams, Fried, 32
Mummy Wrappings, 46–47
Mushrooms
    Triple-Decker Veggie Club, 79
Mustard
    Mustard Sauce, 81
    Spicy Mustard, 42
Mystery Machine Stakeout Snacks menu, 136
Mystery-Solving Dinner Party menu, 136

N

Night Sky Tart, with Bat Cookies, 111–13
Nuts
    Goth Bites, 72–74
    It's a Clue! Panna Cotta, 135
    Scooby Snack Mix, 25
    Werewolf Snacks, Chunky-Style, 31

O

Olives
    Sinister Spaghetti, 59
    Spooky Layer Dip, 35
    Super-Duper Hero Sandwich, 75
    Zucchini Zombies, 49

P

Panna Cotta, It's a Clue!, 135
Pasta. See Spaghetti
Pastries, Headless Horseman, 132
Peaches
    Plain Iced Tea . . . If It Wasn't for You Muddling Kids!!, 103
Peanut butter
    C.R.U.S.T. Sticky Situation, 54
    Eyeball Bites, 45
    Jeepers! It's the Creeper Dog, 66
    Scooby Shake (and Shiver), 88
    Scooby Snacks, 22
    Super Garlic Food, 41
Peanuts
    Scooby Snack Mix, 25
    Werewolf Snacks, Chunky-Style, 31
Pepperoni
    Rizza Rie with Cherry Sauce, 60
Peppers. See also Chili peppers
    Save Breakfast!, 56
    Spooky Layer Dip, 35
    Super-Duper Hero Sandwich, 75
Pesto sandwiches, Dusk's, 74
Pickled Vampire Wings, 30
Pineapple
    Countess Hagula's Youth Juice, 100
Pine nuts
    Dusk's pesto sandwiches, 74
    Luna's blackberry-carrot sandwich, 73
    Thorn's Raspberry Rose Sandwich, 72
Pistachios
    It's a Clue! Panna Cotta, 135
Pizza. See Rizza Rie
Plain Iced Tea . . . If It Wasn't for You Muddling Kids!!, 103
Po' Boy, Hot Pepper, 85

141

Popcorn
  Scooby Snack Mix, 25
  Secret Silo Popcorn, 29
Pork. See also Bacon
  Jaw-Stretcher Special, 82
  Jeepers! It's the Creeper Dog, 66
  Rizza Rie with Cherry Sauce, 60
  Super-Duper Hero Sandwich, 75
Potatoes
  Crawling Potato Beetles, 38
  Finger (and Toe) Fries, 43
  Ghost Pirate Stew, 57
  Save Breakfast!, 56
Pretzels
  Scooby Shake (and Shiver), 88
  Scooby Snack Mix, 25
Prosciutto
  Ham Sandwich (to Calm My Nerves), 81
Protein powder
  Looks Like We Got Ourselves a Protein Shake, 92
Puff pastry
  Headless Horseman Pastries, 132
  Mummy Wrappings, 46–47
  Zucchini Zombies, 49
Puff rice cereal
  Mellow Mutt Munchies, 26
Pumpkin
  Headless Horseman Pastries, 132

R

Raspberry jam
  Bat Macarons, 130–31
  C.R.U.S.T. Sticky Situation, 54
Raspberry-rose sandwich, Thorn's, 72
Relish, Sweet Cherry, 12
Rice cereal
  Mellow Mutt Munchies, 26
Rizza Rie with Cherry Sauce, 60
Rock and Roll Ritual Tea, 101

S

Salads
  Caprese Skull Salad, 40
  Werewolf Snacks, Chunky-Style, 31
Salami
  Super-Duper Hero Sandwich, 75
Salsa, Corn, 65
Sandwiches
  Goth Bites, 72–74
  Ham Sandwich (to Calm My Nerves), 81
  Hot Pepper Po' Boy, 85
  Jaw-Stretcher Special, 82
  Super-Duper Hero Sandwich, 75
  Triple-Decker Veggie Club, 79
Sardines, Chocolate Covered, 15
Sauces
  Bayou Pierre's Hot Sauce, 13
  Crema, 63
  Mustard Sauce, 81
  Sinister Spaghetti, 59
Sausages
  Jaw-Stretcher Special, 82
  Jeepers! It's the Creeper Dog, 66
  Super-Duper Hero Sandwich, 75
Save Breakfast!, 56
Scooby Doo Cookie Tags, 128
Scooby-Doo Watch Party menu, 136
Scooby Shake (and Shiver), 88
Scooby Snack Mix, 25
Scooby Snacks, 22
Seafood
  Creepy Crab Brûlée, 50
  Ghost Pirate Stew, 57
  Hot Pepper Po' Boy, 85
  Rizza Rie with Cherry Sauce, 60
Secret Silo Popcorn, 29
Shakes
  Looks Like We Got Ourselves a Protein Shake, 92
  Scooby Shake (and Shiver), 88
  Zoinks! It's a Shaggy Shake, 91
Shrimp
  Ghost Pirate Stew, 57
  Hot Pepper Po' Boy, 85
Sinister Spaghetti, 59
Skulls, Mozzarella, 19
Skull Salad, Caprese, 40
Sour cream
  Crema, 63
  Werewolf Snacks, Chunky-Style, 31
Spaghetti, Sinister, 59
Spicy Funky Fritters, 42
Spinach
  Dusk's pesto sandwiches, 74
  Triple-Decker Veggie Club, 79
Spooky Haunted House Cake, 115–19
Spooky Layer Dip, 35
Squash. See Pumpkin; Zucchini
Stakeout? I'd Rather Have Steak In!, 62
Stew, Ghost Pirate, 57
Strawberries
  A Trap Cake, 120–23
Super-Duper Hero Sandwich, 75

Super Garlic Food, 41
Sweet Cherry Relish, 12
Syrup, Double Dutch Chocolate, 11

T

Tacos, Hot Dog, with All the Trimmings, 65
Tart, Night Sky, with Bat Cookies, 111–13
Tea
  Jinkies! It's Thai Iced Tea, 96
  Plain Iced Tea . . . If It Wasn't for You Muddling Kids!!, 103
  Rock and Roll Ritual Tea, 101
Thorn's raspberry-rose sandwich, 72
Toadstool Toppers, 16–17
Tomatoes
  Caprese Skull Salad, 40
  Corn Salsa, 65
  Hex Fire Chili, 63
  Hot Pepper Po' Boy, 85
  Jaw-Stretcher Special, 82
  Mini Burgers in a Pile, 69
  Sinister Spaghetti, 59
  Triple-Decker Veggie Club, 79
Toppings
  Bayou Pierre's Hot Sauce, 13
  Chocolate Covered Sardines, 15
  Double Dutch Chocolate Syrup, 11
  Mozzarella Skulls, 19
  Sweet Cherry Relish, 12
  Toadstool Toppers, 16–17
Tortillas
  Chili Snacks, 29
  Hot Dog Tacos with All the Trimmings, 65
  Spooky Layer Dip, 35
A Trap Cake, 120–23
Triple-Decker Veggie Club, 79
Turkey
  Super-Duper Hero Sandwich, 75

V

Vampire Wings, Pickled, 30

W

Werewolf Snacks, Chunky-Style, 31
White chocolate
  Like, It's Green, Like My Favorite Shirt, 99
  Toadstool Toppers, 16–17

Z

Zoinks! It's a Shaggy Shake, 91
Zucchini Zombies, 49

About the Authors

Elena Pons Craig is a food and prop stylist and recipe developer with more than 25 years of experience in culinary design, marketing, photography, and publishing. With a deep love for pop culture, she enjoys hiding Easter eggs in depictions of fictional worlds. With her husband and two children, she has developed superhero cooking skills that cross generations, genders, and genres.

"I want to thank my kids, August and Jac, for being a constant source of ideas and inspiration. My husband, mother, and friends for all the taste-testing. A special thanks to Marc for working on this with me and to Anna and Sami who make the best editing team. To Patricia, thank you for always saying, 'Yes, we can do that,' whenever I suggest something crazy and for your amazing decorating skills that bring my visions to life." — Elena

Marc Sumerak is an Eisner and Harvey Awards–nominated writer and editor whose work over the past two decades has been featured in comics, books, and video games showcasing some of pop culture's most beloved franchises, including Marvel, *Star Wars*, Harry Potter, Back to the Future, and many more. He is based in Cleveland, Ohio.

"I would like to thank my own personal Scooby Gang — Elena, Sami, and Anna — for letting me tag along on the tastiest case ever! Thanks to Charlie and Lincoln for never passing up on a snack, an adventure, or a chance to get into trouble ("ruh roh!"). Thanks to Indiana for being the best pup a guy could ever hope to have (sorry, Scoob!). And, of course, to all our snacking sleuths out there: Bon Appétit!" — Marc

PO Box 3088
San Rafael, CA 94912
www.insighteditions.com

Find us on Facebook: www.facebook.com/InsightEditions
Follow us on Instagram: @insighteditions

 Copyright © 2025 Hanna-Barbera. SCOOBY-DOO and all related characters and elements © & ™ Hanna-Barbera. WB SHIELD: © & ™ WBEI. (s25)

No part of this book may be reproduced in any form without written permission from the publisher.

ISBN: 979-8-88663-928-5

Publisher: Raoul Goff
SVP, Group Publisher: Vanessa Lopez
VP, Creative: Chrissy Kwasnik
VP, Manufacturing: Alix Nicholaeff
Publishing Director: Mike Degler
Editorial Director: Thom O'Hearn
Art Director: Stuart Smith
Senior Designer: Judy Wiatrek Trum
Assistant Editor: Sami Alvarado
Managing Editor: Shannon Ballesteros
Production Manager: Deena Hashem
Strategic Production Planner: Lina s Palma-Temena

Photographer: Ted Thomas
Food & Prop Stylist: Elena P. Craig
Lead Decorator & Assistant Food Stylist: Patricia C Parrish
Assistant Food Stylist: Lauren Tedeschi

Insight Editions, in association with Roots of Peace, will plant two trees for each tree used in the manufacturing of this product.

Manufactured in China by Insight Editions

10 9 8 7 6 5 4 3 2 1

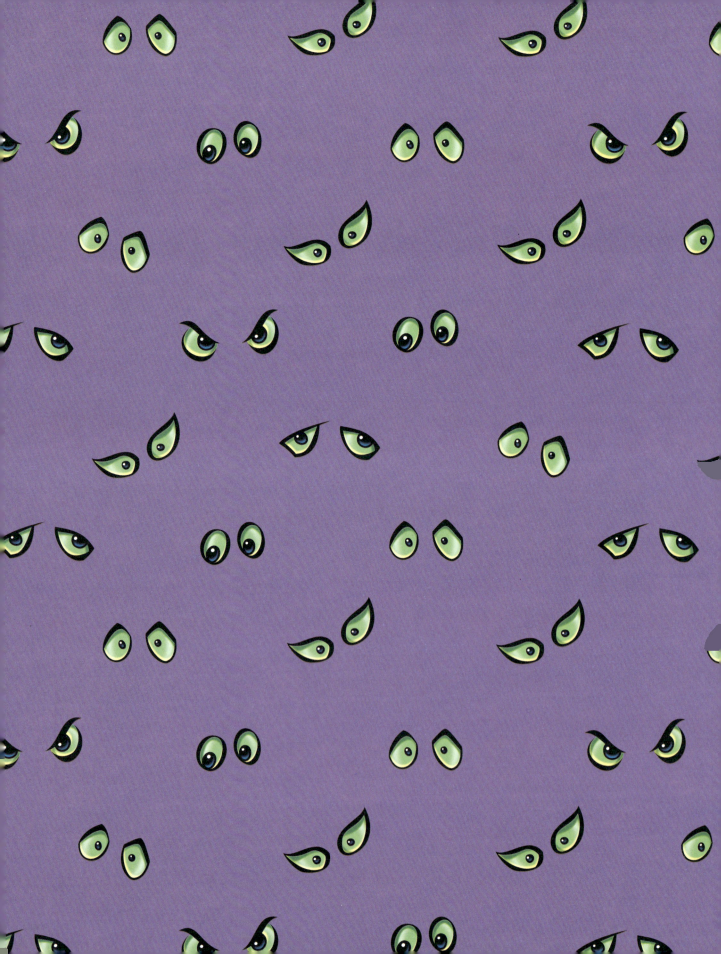